Walks in
MYSTERIOUS
DEVON

Trevor Beer

Published by Sigma Leisure – an imprint of Sigma Press, 1 South Oak Lane, Wilmslow, Cheshire SK9 6AR, England.

British Library Cataloguing in Publication Data
A CIP record for this book is available from the British Library.

ISBN: 1-85058-607-1

Typesetting and Design by: Sigma Press, Wilmslow, Cheshire.

Cover photograph: Trees near Swincombe, Exmoor *(the author)*

Maps and Photographs: the author

Printed by: MFP Design and Print

Disclaimer: the information in this book is given in good faith and is believed to be correct at the time of publication. No responsibility is accepted by either the author or publisher for errors or omissions, or for any loss or injury howsoever caused. Only you can judge your own fitness, competence and experience.

Preface

This is a book of country walks in Devon, including Dartmoor and Exmoor – the latter occasionally having its borders with Somerset crossed of necessity. Take these walks in the true spirit of the countryside. Enjoy the mud on your boots as being of Mother Earth, letting an open mind guide you where the past, present and future mingles and merges in ways we may not always understand.

Be on the lookout for ghosts and other mysterious creatures and happenings of the highways and byways, for these walks are specially chosen for their links with hauntings and other aspects of the unexplained.

Occasionally in such places mists fall suddenly, and weather conditions change dramatically, especially on the moors and coast. Wear sensible clothing including stout footwear, preferably with ankle protection, and carry a waterproof and warm jumper. Remember to take plenty of fluids in order to avoid dehydration.

The walks vary in length and terrain. Some are very easy, but adhere to common sense safety rules at all times and avoid risks. If in doubt, let someone know where you are heading, timing yourself to avoid nightfall catching you out in remote places.

Walks are not timed. Pace varies greatly and some will pause to watch birds or look at flowers, or ghosts. Gauge your own timing using the distances shown. A small pack is useful with maybe a drink, an apple or a chocolate bar and a walker's first-aid kit. Add to these a map, a compass, and perhaps a torch, binoculars or a camera for those memories. I always take a walking stick or thumbstick on all walks. Good luck and happy times.

Dedication

To Bracken, our dog, who takes me walking, and to Shepherd before him.

Devon: Location Map

Contents

Beyond Exmoor and Dartmoor

Rainy Day Walking

Mysterious Bits and Pieces

Of Country Lore and Legend

The walker in Devon will soon become aware that here is a county rich in different habitats. There is a lovely mix of moorland, estuaries, rivers and streams, patchwork farmland and forestry, rugged coastlines, woodlands and old country lanes – each supporting a rich variety of flora and fauna species. England's pastures green!

It is thought by some that Jesus may have walked here, and Joseph of Arimathea; the geographer Ptolemy wrote in about AD100 that Hercules settled for a while at Hartland Point after sailing to Devon in a golden bowl. It is also said that Conan Doyle's *Hound of the Baskervilles* may owe its ancestry to the phantom Black Dogs of Dartmoor; and that the robber Doones of Exmoor and the Gubbins of Dartmoor have their basis in fact as much as legend.

Devon, like the rest of the West Country, is steeped in folklore. Fairies and pixies live here along with witches aplenty. It is a magical place and walking is the best way to enjoy it, perhaps. To avoid being pixie-led or disorientated by pixies on Dartmoor, wear your coat back to front when on the moor. If this leads to reports of strange, faceless creatures walking the moors backwards then so be it – this is the stuff of mystery and enchantment!

So let us walk first on the great and beautiful moors of Devonshire, Dartmoor and Exmoor, remembering that they of all places are perhaps more liable to changes in the conditions of the terrain, especially seasonal differences such as those of higher water table in winter, for example. Such changes can alter the timing of a walk, even doubling the time, as well as increasing the risks of a soaking. So always heed the advice in the Preface and be safe, not sorry.

Tourist Information for Walkers in Devon

Local telephone directories have extensive listings of Dartmoor and Exmoor National Park Offices, Tourism Information Centres for Devon and other helpful contacts in the county who may be 'walker friendly'.

A Devonshire sunset: prelude to a ghostly encounter?

Dartmoor

Devon without Sir Francis Drake would be like Devon without clotted cream or dumplings, and thankfully all three can be found on Dartmoor, the latter two as part of the fare to enjoy *en route.*

Drake, as well as being a British naval hero, remains the cause of even stranger events than sea battles for his ghost is still said to roam the moor, riding with a pack of spectral hounds whose cries are so terrible that any dog hearing them dies on the spot. Another legend says he rides in a black coach drawn by headless horses, sometimes preceded by goblins with flashing eyes and smoke issuing from their nostrils.

How could anyone resist walking across mysterious Dartmoor knowing there is a good chance of such sightings? And maybe we'll find Drake on the circular walk from Widecombe and on to Hameldon Beacon and Grimspound, about 8 miles and worth every footstep. Let's go.

Walk 1: Widecombe-in-the Moor to Grimspound and back

Grid Reference: SX 719768

Distance: 8 miles (11km)

Terrain: Rugged but not difficult. Steep in places.

Refreshments: At starting point.

Starting Point: Widecombe-in-the-Moor

Begin at The Old Inn, itself haunted by at least two ghosts, though one named Harry is said to have left following a fire in 1977. Evidently he was murdered here and his ghost used to be seen in the kitchen. And if you hear the sobbing of a young woman from an upstairs room, you could be hearing Kitty Day who hanged herself here in the 18th century.

Widecombe, is well known, of course, for its famous fair held each September, and for Bill Brewer, Jan Stewer, Uncle Tom Cobleigh and all, from the folk song of *Widecombe Fair*. These are legendary, but real characters, the "Uncle Tom" of the song was probably he who died in 1794 and was buried at Spreyton in Devon in an unmarked grave. (Spreyton is 12 miles [16½km] north of Wide-combe.) The lofty-towered church at Widecombe is locally called the cathedral of Dartmoor.

From the inn go left, then turn left to the lane leading to Natsworthy. About 200 metres along, turn left and follow the path signposted to Hameldown and Grimspound. Go through a gate ahead and take the path across the moor, keeping a stone wall on your right. When the wall bears right, go straight on along the wide, grassy pathway. (Do not deviate onto the path crossing your way here.)

Now ignore the lane and bear right, uphill to Hameldon Beacon. Broad Barrow is here, and less than 400 metres north-west is the Hameldon Cross, about 120cm (4ft) in height and of granite. Initials carved in the cross refer to its own name and 'D.S.' for the Duke of

Somerset who owned the nearby Natsworthy estate. There is also the date, 1854. Just due south of Broad Barrow is Single Barrow.

From Hameldon Beacon, Mis Tor and Cut Hill (west-north-west) can be located. Due south is Brent Hill, whilst eastward lie the tors, Honeybag and Chinkwell, with Hound Tor, Hey Tor and Rippon Tor beyond.

The Wild Hunt or Demon Hunt may be about this area, the Demon Huntsman having been seen at this very spot. A man returning from Widecombe fair to Chagford one stormy night met the Wild Hunt on Hamel Down. Jet black hounds with glowing eyes were followed by the Demon Hunter on a jet black horse. He called to the huntsman for some of his game, asking him what sport he had had. The huntsman replied, 'Take that,' and threw a parcel at the man. The man took the parcel home and unwrapping it in his courtyard, found to his horror the body of his own small child.

The Wild Hunt has its origins in Norse traditions. Before Christianity came to Britain it was thought that Odin the Norse god chased across the night skies with a pack of baying hounds at his horse's heels. A bad omen, indeed, to see or speak to the huntsman. With Christianity arriving, so Odin's place was taken by the Devil. Christian leaders of the time were quick to exploit folklore, be it fact or fiction, to bring people to follow Christianity as quickly as possible.

Whether you will hang about to make positive identification if you meet with the Wild Hunt remains to be seen! It is said in some parts that if a child dies before he or she has had a chance to be baptised then the child will turn into a butterfly. A lovely legend, but in Devon the story is that the child is hunted by the Wild Hunt and will turn into another Yeth Hound, to hunt forever across Dartmoor.

Enjoy the primitive moorland hereabouts with its relics of Stone Age man, splashing streams and ghostly spirits, then move on left along the ridge, passing Broad Barrow towards Hameldon Tor. Now go downhill to the 1.6 hectares (4 acre) circular enclosure of Grimspound itself. The stream flowing through the enclosure is the Grimslake. Look for the entrance (south-south-east) which still shows signs of paving. Grimspound is thought to have been a cattle pound and there are 24 hut circles within its walls.

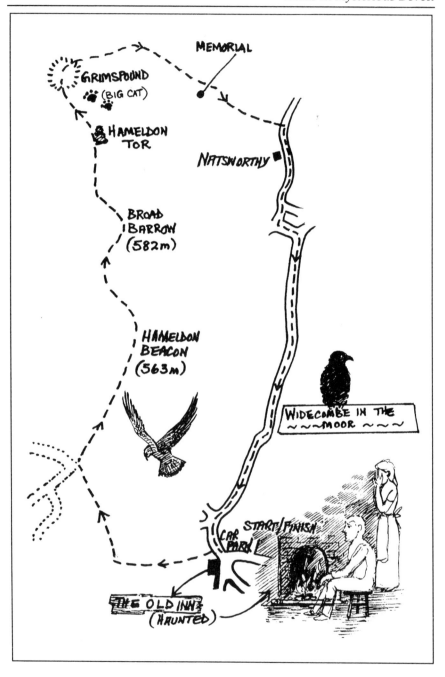

Out of Grimslake, turn right along a sandy track, passing the World War II memorial stone to the crew of an RAF Bomber which crashed here in 1941. Bear right along a road, passing Natsworthy Manor on your right. This road takes you back to Widecombe.

As if to add credence to the tales of black hounds and such haunting the moors here, it was in 1996 that an army officer and his wife saw a "huge black cat, a panther" sitting in the sunshine within Grimspound on a June day. They watched it from the hillside above for some time, using binoculars, then, deciding it seemed docile, went to have a closer look. When they entered Grimspound the animal had vanished from where they were positive it had been basking. They did not see it again nor did they hang about in order to do so!

Note: The Dewerstone Rock is an interesting geological feature with the vertical jointing very marked. 'Dewer' in Dewerstone is said by some to mean 'stone by the water', by others 'rock of the pigeons', but there it rests awaiting a decision or new ideas. Golden eagles have been traditionally associated with Dartmoor, with old reports of the species nesting on the Dewerstone though ornithologists have argued that the eagles seen there were of the white-tailed race. A good natural history legend, however, though today people pressure would hardly allow eagles to nest on lovely Dartmoor.

Sir Francis Drake's drum is at Buckland Abbey, his old home, and is said to sound when the nation is in trouble. As to the game of bowls he is said to have been playing when news of the Spanish Armada reached him, old records state the game was 'kales', a form of skittles.

Walk 2: Belstone - Steeperton Tor - Cosdon Hill

Grid Reference: SX 619936

Distance: 10 miles (6km)

Terrain: Tough going with some ascents. Not a bad weather walk.

Refreshments: Belstone

Starting Point: Belstone village

A wild walk which ought not to be risked in bad weather, and one needs to check Ministry of Defence firing activities as the route between Knattaborough and Steeperton Tor is within the Okehampton firing range.

Belstone village is an excellent starting point, even retaining its stocks on the village green in readiness for unruly walkers! Against the wall of the church is an old grave cover with an incised cross

Belstone stocks

forming part of the design carved into the stone. This was found in 1861 during alterations to steps in the vestry area.

Walk from the village centre, keeping the Tors Inn on the left and the old post office on the right. Take the left fork just up the hill (not the turning on the left to the church). The way is signed 'Dartmoor – No through Road'. Go by the Belstone Treatment Works on the right and through the moor gate at Watchet, going straight on along the track with the stone wall on your right. Where the track divides go left, and after some 50 metres go half-left to the Nine Maidens prehistoric standing stones.

If you arrive here at noon you may see 'the maidens' dancing, but do not worry that there are not 9 in number. There are other Nine Maidens sites, often with more or less than that number of stones, and some say it is a reference to 'noon' which was our 3pm or the ninth hour of the day in Roman and ecclesiastical terms. A church service called Nones was moved to midday, with 'noon' remaining in our language to mean just that today. More likely it has to do with the Great Earth Mother goddess who was, and is, deified here by white witches who regard Nine Maidens as three deities – aspects of the moon, each with three aspects, making nine goddesses or maidens. Legend has it that the maidens were dancing here on the sabbath and turned to stone for doing so.

Dowsing here shows alternating negative and positive stones. Dancing in and out of these in a circle, as carried out by white witches, raised a 'cone' or pyramid of earth energy at these powerful ley sites, which was dispersed for the purpose of healing and good – something like a dynamo. Another theory is that they are named from Maiden Nun, meaning moorland stones.

However, I subscribe to dancing on the 'sabbath' as referring to sabbat, and not to Sundays at all, and believe the punishment theory was suggested by Christians pursuing their anti-pagan propaganda some 1500 years ago in Britain.

On with the walk. Go straight on uphill to Tors End. This is the northernmost outcrop on Watchet Hill, marking the beginning of the Belstone Tors. Go around the east (left) side of the Tor where you will find considerable evidence of stone cutting. Now go straight on

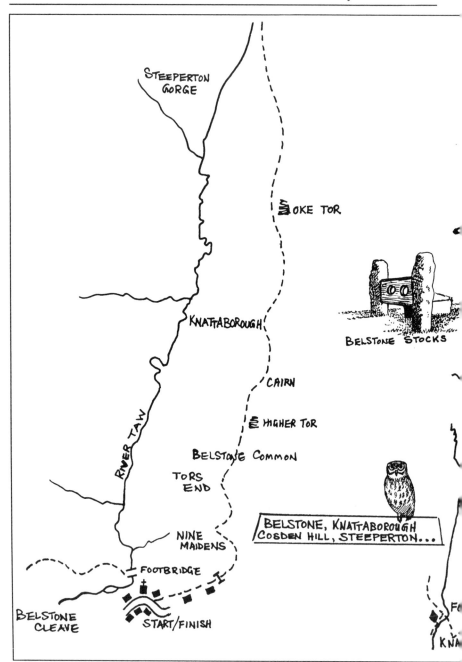

STEEPERTON
GORGE

OKE TOR

KNATTABOROUGH

BELSTONE STOCKS

CAIRN

HIGHER TOR

RIVER TAW

BELSTONE COMMON

TORS
END

BELSTONE, KNATTABOROUGH
COSDEN HILL, STEEPERTON...

NINE
MAIDENS

FOOTBRIDGE

BELSTONE
CLEAVE

START/FINISH

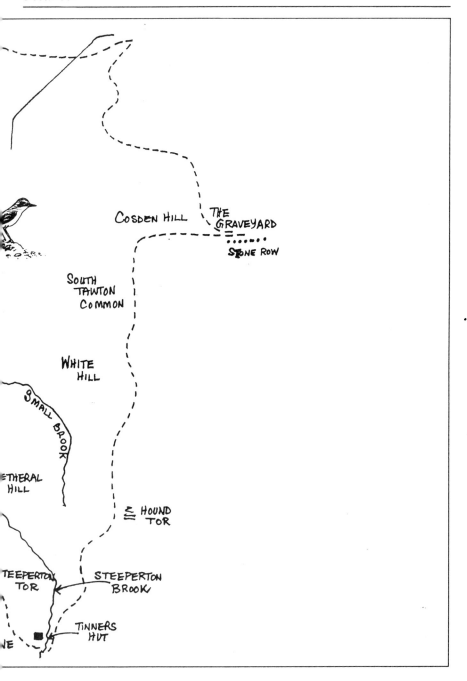

up to the next outcrop, keeping to the right path for this Tor, then straight along the ridge crest going round the left side of Belstone Tor. Here various shrubs and other vegetation grow in profusion, and during 1996 we saw both merlin and ring ouzel at this point.

From Higher Tor go down to two boundary stones then bear right, passing a grass-covered cairn, and on along the ridge to the next outcrop which is Knattaborough. You are now on the Okehampton firing range. If you hear firing and yet have checked to see it is a non-firing day, this will be training with blanks. Go along the grassy track to Oke Tor for fine views of High Willhays (621 metres) and Yes Tor (619 metres). You may not like the obvious military use of the moor, the very visual tracks and such, but believe me there could be far worse intrusions, such as 4-wheel drive buggies and similar as tourist attractions. I have heard this idea being put forward! The military presence has its plus side and is arguably better than many uses where wildlife is concerned.

Go straight on along the track to a ford across the River Taw and keeping the river on the left, go upstream along the path for about 150 metres to the long disused Knack Mine, a 19th-century tin mine. Go back to the river and re-cross it, going on upstream for a few paces then take the path left which takes you up to Steeperton Tor, aiming for the look-out hut.

Go right from the hut to the South outcrop, then follow a narrow path half-left towards Wild Tor, going on down to the ford over Steeperton Brook. Keep on the left side of the waterway downstream for 50 metres to a ruined tinner's house for a browse. Now go back and cross the river, and just up the hill go left down a well-used track, continuing on past Hound Tor on your right. Where the track divides go right to the White Moor Stone Circle. There are balanced rocks on Hound Tor, whilst midway between the tor and the road is a 'closed' stone circle of a more unusual kind. The White Moor Stone itself is a flat slab about 1.8 metres (6ft) in height, some 150 metres south-south-east of the circle.

Here also is an upright bondstone and cairn. Now retrace your steps to where the track divides, ignoring the bridlepath to the left and right, and go along the path which leads over the hill of Little

Hound Tor, continuing straight up to the cairn-topped summit of Cosdon Hill.

Go on to the northern most cairn. Turn right downhill, where the path is ill-defined and may be rough going. As the slope levels out, aim for the triple stone row near the head of Cheriton Combe on the right. (This stone row dowses to being over 4000 years old.)

At the nearest end of the stone row, bear half-left up through bracken to contour round the north-east side of Cosdon Hill, keeping well to the left of the bondstone on South Zeal common close to Foxes' Holt. An odd mix! Foxes live in earths, otters in holts. At the well-defined bridlepath, turn right and go down to its junction with another. Turn left to go on over the channel of an old leat, heading for beautiful Belstone Cleave down on your right. Yes, this is the Belstone of *The Belstone Fox* story by the way. You must pause here to take in the wonderful views right across mid-Devon. Go on down to the valley bottom, cross the footbridge and continue up the hillside to Belstone village.

Note: The Irishman's Wall is said to have been built by Irish men directed by one Matthew Crawford, a moorland land-grabber. The locals drove the immigrants away, refusing to have Dartmoor put in bounds in that way.

Walk 3: Merrivale, King's Tor, Swell Tor and Foggin Tor

Grid Reference: SX 553750

Distance: 4 miles (6.5km)

Terrain: Quite level for Dartmoor. Chosen as an easy, short walk.

Refreshments: Dartmoor Inn, near to starting point

Starting Point: Merrivale car park, in a quarry left of B3357

For those interested in prehistoric stone rows, menhirs, cairns and other standing stones, Merrivale is the perfect place. One could spend a hundred happy hours here just wandering about and drinking in the very essence of Dartmoor.

The essence of the mysterious is, of course, a main ingredient of our walks and it is Merrivale Bridge and nearby Vixen Tor that were home to an extremely evil black witch who would perch high on the Tor to cast her spells, bringing about dense mists which caused travellers to become lost, doomed to be killed in the moorland bogs. Eventually, a moorman who had been befriended by pixies made himself invisible using a magic ring they had given him, and creeping up behind her he pushed her from the summit into the bog below.

In *Traditions of Devonshire*, Mrs Bray reports on a tradition that certain of the stone circles at Merrivale Bridge were used as a plague market during an epidemic in the 17th century. With the plague raging in Tavistock, people from surrounding villages left their goods in the circles and the Tavistock residents collected them and left payment. In this way, the villagers hoped to avoid catching the terrible disease. For many years the stone circles were known as the Potato Market, and money for goods was left in bowls of water.

So an interesting place to begin and end our walk. From the east end of the car park, with your back to Merrivale quarry, go over the moor half-right towards North Hessary Tor mast. After about 230

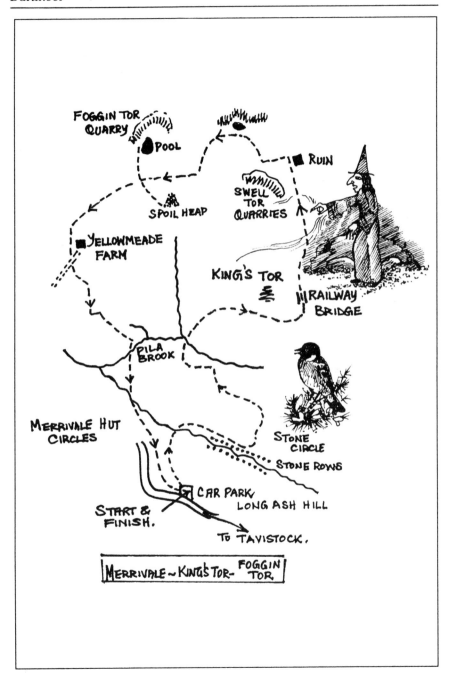

FOGGIN TOR QUARRY

POOL

RUIN

SWELL TOR QUARRIES

SPOIL HEAP

YELLOWMEADE FARM

KING'S TOR

RAILWAY BRIDGE

PILA BROOK

MERRIVALE HUT CIRCLES

STONE CIRCLE

STONE ROWS

CAR PARK

LONG ASH HILL

START & FINISH.

TO TAVISTOCK.

MERRIVALE ~ KING'S TOR - FOGGIN TOR.

Merrivale and ponies

metres, go half-right again over Long Ash Hill, with some fine views
of a stone circle, a menhir, three stone rows and some cairns.

Keep to the left of the rows and go over a leat using the granite
slab put there for the purpose. Follow the southern double stone row
down due west to the far end, about 260 metres, and go half-left
passing a cairn circle. Go to the menhir and bear left, keeping the
wall on the right, to follow the path. Keep above left of the bluff for
a short distance then go down right to follow the path through spoil
heaps, keeping the stream on the right. Cross the stream, which is
the Pila Brook, by the ford and go on along the boundary wall up
the slope on your right. Where the wall goes sharp right, go straight
on up the hill to pick up the track of the old Princetown and
Yelverton Railway. This track forks as it goes left round King's Tor.
Take the right fork for fine views of the Walkham Valley and follow
the track left. Go on the granite rail bridge, cross over the track and
then go right for Swell Tor sidings. Go on along the track to Swell
Tor Quarry, but be careful of old rail sleepers and such. From the
old building on the right, opposite the quarry entrance, turn left
uphill, keeping the quarry entrance down to your left and staying

well away from the quarry edge. Half way up the hill bear right past spoil heaps and continue along the track curving to the left, passing quarries and spoil heaps on the right. Go on towards Foggintor quarries and where the path crosses with another, turn right and go towards the quarries. You will reach the P & Y rail track here in a shallow cutting. Go straight across and continue on. At the next track bear left to some ruined buildings. At the largest ruin bear left between the two walls of the building and follow the spoil heap to its furthest end, again watching the way for protruding ironwork.

You now have excellent views of Cox Tor, King's Tor, Staple Tor, Roos Tor and Great Mis Tor, whilst below lies Yellowmeade Farm. Go back to the track and take the path leading into the quarry, with a lake. Buzzards and ravens may well be here and some say they come here in the stillness and solitude and have actually heard the old sounds of quarrying and men's voices haunting the site.

Go back to the track and right along it, passing Yellowmeade Farm on your left. On reaching the last stone-walled enclosure on your left, go straight on for 20 metres beyond the junction with the farm track. Go left past an oval enclosure and downhill to the standing stone marking an ancient way over the moor.

Go half-right and continue on towards Four Winds, a lone clump of beech trees, to cross over gullies, then a small stream to go on over the hill towards Great Staple Tor, keeping Four Winds to your right. Cross over the leat and keeping it on your left, go on to the stone rows once more then bear half-right towards Merrivale Quarry. Find the Tavistock to Ashburton marker stone on the left, in line with King's Tor. Go half-right by some hut circles and straight on towards Merrivale Quarry and the car park.

Walk 4: Okehampton Castle, Meldon Reservoir and Bracken Tor

Grid Reference: SX 586945

Distance: 6 miles (9km) – shorter option

Terrain: Rugged moorland, not difficult. See warning below.

Refreshments: At start and finish (Okehampton).

Starting Point: From the hospital area after visiting Okehampton Castle.

The walk from Okehampton Castle to Meldon Reservoir and back via Okehampton Park and Bracken Tor (about 5 miles) can be extended by walking from the reservoir to Yes Tor and taking in High Willhays (about 6 miles).

Taken as two walks, the first is easy, the second stunningly beautiful for its wildness but best not taken in bad weather conditions. Please heed this warning and also the fact that the extended walk enters the Okehampton MOD firing range so firing times must be checked. (Tel. 01837 52241)

Okehampton Castle is close to the town, which has excellent facilities including food and refreshments, good pubs etc. The Castle is an imposing ruin, ideal for photography or as an artist's subject. It is certainly deserving of an hour or two for exploration. Originally there was a market and park adjoining the Castle, which looks one way to fertile farmland, the other to the rugged outlines of the moor.

The River Okement, once the Uisz maenic or 'stony water', gives its name to Okehampton.

Our interest in the mysterious here is linked with Fitzford House, near Tavistock, which is haunted by Lady Howard whose life was eventful and tragic in the 17th century. She rides the moor in a coach made of human bones with skulls at the four corners which is drawn by headless horses. The coach is accompanied by a black dog, or dogs, said to have only one eye in the middle of the forehead.

An old poem says:

"I'd rather walk a hundred miles,
And run by night and day,
Than have that carriage halt for me,
And hear my Lady say -
Now pray step in and make no din,
Step in with me to ride;
There's room, I trow, by me for you,
And all the world beside."

The dog has the onerous task of plucking one blade of grass each night from the mound of Okehampton Castle and carrying it to the gate at Fitzford, and must do so until all have been plucked.

Okehampton Castle

Okehampton also comes under the ghostly spotlight with former Mayor Benjamin Gayer who, as one of his duties, administered a fund for ransoming Christian sailors from the Turks. It is said the Turks captured several merchant ships belonging to Gayer who, faced with ruin, reimbursed himself from the fund. When he died his restless spirit haunted Okehampton and became such a nuisance that 23 clergymen were asked to exorcise it. They were not successful until one requested it in Arabic, at which the spirit acknowledged defeat and turned into an unbroken colt. An expert

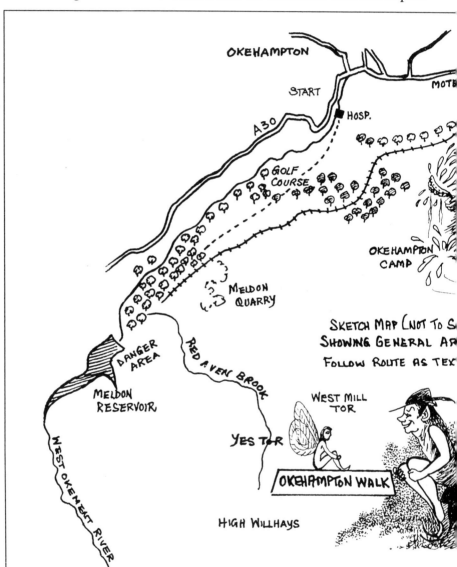

horseman took the Holy Sacrament, mounted the colt and galloped off across Dartmoor to Cranmere Pool, the source of the River Taw. Here the horseman leapt off and the colt galloped on to be drowned. Some tales say the colt vanished in a ball of fire, but not before it lashed out with its hooves to knock out one of its rider's eyes.

FOR WALK 4.
REFULLY . . .

So, lots to think about on the walk which, after visiting Okehampton Castle, begins on a signposted footpath by the hospital which is clearly shown on OS maps. Follow the path south off the road and through a pleasant wooded area with the West Okement river on your right. At a crossroads on the path go south-west into lovely, open countryside over the Okehampton Golf Course area (Pathfinder Map SX49/59), between the river and the railway. The route veers gradually south and enters woods close to the river until you go under Meldon Viaduct. Continue south to a right-hand turning to the well-signposted reservoir.

If you are doing the extended walk, leave the National Park Authority car park and picnic area, pass the information board and toilet block and go through the gate. Turn left and follow the lane to the dam and cross it. Here are dramatic views over the drowned valley and Meldon Quarry, a British Rail ballast quarry, as well as the viaduct. Go through the gate at the end of the dam and walk left through another gate and down the steps to the dam base.

Walk downstream on the right bank

and cross the Red-a-ven Brook close to its confluence with the West Okement. After the brook go straight on, ignoring the right- hand track, and after some 45 metres turn left and go over a wooden bridge spanning the West Okement. Here you can view a drowned limestone quarry before going back over the bridge and going left along the path. Keep the river on the left as you go down towards the viaduct, past a disused building (at the time of writing) to a telegraph pole. Follow the path round to the left and head for the large quarry opening. Keeping this on the opposite side of the Red-a-ven Brook, walk on up the valley past a huge, walled construction and then a smaller quarry on the left.

Go upstream with the river to the right, passing the waterfalls and pools on you way to the Firing Range notice board. Cross the stream, the Nether Brook, and go straight on. Follow on along the Red-a-ven, staying close to the river as the valley closes in.

Follow the rather ill-defined path and the valley opens out with a stream forming from a spring up ahead on the left. Go above the spring to avoid swampy ground and continue half-right to rejoin the riverbank near Yes Tor Ford. Carry on upstream without crossing the river.

You are now in much steeper country – climb on up to the small dam which impounds the Red-a-ven Brook, forming a deep pool. Cross the river here and go on upstream with the river on the left. Near the river source the brook is more a stream, though heavy rains tend to make the waterway a torrent. The drier ground is close to the river. Continue on, a low bluff is on your right. Go right and above the bluff for Yes Tor summit. To avoid a scramble up the massive clitter slope, go round to the left to ascend the final uphill to the summit. The views are extensive and include parts of Cornwall and Somerset. A stone cairn, now ruined, lies on the north-west side of the Tor here.

Go due south along the ridge top to the smaller outcrops of High Willhays and head along a track to the military lookout hut and stable of Fordsland hedge. Some of the wildest scenery on Dartmoor is before you. Turn right at the hut and pass a prehistoric cairn. Continue on, bearing slightly left, then go down the heather and grass slope to Black Tor and its three granite piles. Aim for the southernmost (first) pile and pass a range notice board. Continue straight on to the centre pile, then make for the final outcrop and walk half-right to find an obvious vehicle track across Longstone Hill. This takes you to Meldon Reservoir so walk down the slope for the dam and car park.

Note: Reservoir facts. The dam is 201 metres long and 44 metres high. The reservoir covers 23 hectares. The maximum water depth is 40 metres and the maximum capacity 3000 million litres, supplying a population of 200 000 between Tavistock in the south and Bideford in the north.

High Willhays is 621 metres (1993ft) above sea level, the highest land in England south of Kinder Scout in the Peak District which is 636 metres (2084ft).

For a slightly different walk back to Okehampton, take the route you walked to Meldon Reservoir back through the woods with the West Okement now on your left. Then go along the public path across the fields until you reach a narrow road (573933) leading south-east. This takes you towards Black Down, but take the sharp left-hand turn about 650 metres along this road and follow the public path north-east between the railway and Okehampton camp. The path passes Moor Cottage and goes through Okehampton Park and some woods then bears left to hit the road over the railway and so back to the area of the hospital and our starting point. Enjoy a well-deserved rest and refreshments in the town.

Walk 5: Lydford Castle, Lydford Gorge, The White Lady and Devil's Cauldron

Grid Reference: SX 510847

Distance: 3½ miles (5km)

Terrain: Easy but hilly. All well-maintained footpaths.

Refreshments: Pubs at Lydford, plus shops and the National Trust shop at Lydford Gorge.

Starting Point: Lydford Castle

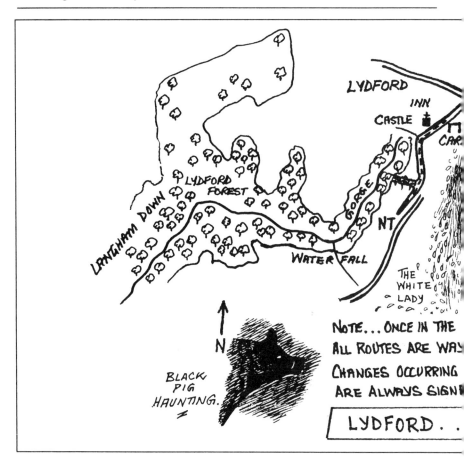

Lydford Castle (NT, seasonal opening April – October) is by the church and close to a good inn and car park. Such a wealth of history and mystery here, even the inn named The Castle was used as The Admiral Blake in *The Hound of the Baskervilles* film. Indeed, there are further Conan Doyle connections on Dartmoor as we shall see.

Do take a look around the castle or keep (1195) which was used to imprison offenders against Forest and Stannary Laws, with links to the infamous 'Hanging Judge' Jeffreys, whose notoriety is remembered throughout the West Country.

The ghost of a young man clad in 17th-century clothes has been seen on the staircase here in recent times. The Keep has such a reputation for hauntings as to have attracted visits from members of the British Psychic and Occult Society here in the 1980s, 'protected' by an alsatian. A brief report from the BPOS President is to be found at the rear of the book.

START & FINISH.

LYDFORD EST.

2KED.

TO PATH REPAIRS

Down the road from the keep is St Petroc's Church on your right with its exhibition on Lydford and its great historical interest. It is worth a pause here.

Walk downhill and over the bridge crossing the River Lyd to the National Trust entrance to Lydford Gorge. An entrance fee is payable if you are not a member but this is too good a walk to miss, with a wealth of wildlife to enjoy. Follow the NT way-marked routes. I suggest the 'long and easy' rather than the 'short and hard', though if you are here for the day you can wander at will.

The White Lady Fall or cascade is magnificent, a 90ft (30m) drop of white water falling out of wooded cliffs to the pool below. Again we are in haunted territory for it is said that those who fall into the swift-flowing river will be saved from drowning if the White Lady herself appears to them. And if that isn't enough, remember Judge Jeffreys. For his brutality in conducting the Bloody Assize following the Monmouth Rebellion he is said to have haunted the West Country as a black boar or pig.

Now for a true story to set you thinking. During my investigation of the so-called 'Beast of Exmoor' and mysterious big cats and other creatures in Britain, I received a letter from a farmer on Dartmoor. He stated that he was at the Lydford Gorge area, at the western end of the Coryhill Plantation, just after sunset, when a strange black creature came towards him from the shadows, snuffling as it came, head held low to the ground. He told me the animal was not a dog but was of labrador size. The farmer said he felt unable to move and watched transfixed in the now dark shadows as the creature walked up to him, literally bumped into his leg, and stopped! He could just make out a short-eared head, dull, red eyes, and a snout! The animal then turned away, walked to a stone wall and climbed over to disappear into trees on the other side. The farmer's letter asked if I thought the Exmoor Beast could have moved to Dartmoor. He said he wondered if it was blind, or near blind, as it walked into him.

I visited the area. The stone wall was 3ft in height, and the farmer said the animal definitely put up its forelegs then climbed over it. A strange method for a dog, cat or pig to use? Dull, red eyes? The farmer was not carrying a torch to reflect in any creature's eyes. Then again a blind, badly-sighted or very old animal may clamber over an obstacle. A snout? Pig-like at least. But more intriguing, when I asked if the bump on contact was hard he told me not, it stopped exactly at his leg and he couldn't really recall the impact. He said he, the farmer, just felt icy cold and could not move until the creature was out of sight. Keep your eyes open.

Cross the bridge over the Lyd by the waterfall, walking upstream with the waterway on your right. Passing a footbridge on your right, carry on to the next and follow the path left above the river to the Devil's Cauldron. Be careful here, a plank causeway takes you to this maelstrom of water with its roar and spray, a wonderfully atmospheric spot which is not to be missed.

You must retrace your steps here, then go left uphill to the main entrance and left back to the village. Other items of interest here include an ancient spring and remains of Lydford's Saxon defences, plus some specimen coins of the time when Ethelred the Unready had them minted here of Dartmoor silver.

Walk 6: Hay Tor and Hound Tor

Grid Reference: SX 754764

Distance: 6½ miles (10km)

Terrain: Some steep ascents.

Refreshments: None

Starting Point: Car park on the east side of Saddle Tor.

The car park on the east side of Saddle Tor (754764) is just off the main Bovey Tracey to Widecombe-in-the-Moor road. Face Hay Tor and walk uphill from the rear of the car park in the direction of a clearly visible, upright bondstone. Go over the brow of the hill where you will see several small, disused quarries. Go right along a path which goes close to the road then up the south side of the Lower Man. Keep Lower Man to your left and turn left between the two bosses of the Tor then half-right to find a well-defined path down to the fenced-in Haytor Quarries. Just before a granite post and some Scots pines you will reach a track. Go left to the workings and follow the perimeter fence downhill. At the bottom of the slope go left and pick upon the granite tramway, or railway as it is sometimes called. Follow the tramway, passing a set of granite points, until you reach a junction between this, the branch line, and the main line to Holwell Tor. In the summer months of 1994-6, a puma was seen by several eyewitnesses in this area..

Turn left at the junction and follow the tramway through a shallow cutting down to the terminal and the sheer, worked face of Holwell Quarry for good photographs. Retrace your steps back up the tramway to a ruined building on the right and a set of granite points. Keep to the left fork to the next set of points, close to some mountain ash or rowan trees. Here follow the narrow path on the left which takes you to the summit of Smallacombe Rocks with magnificent views of the lovely Becka Brook valley. Go on over the summit and bear half-left on a path to the valley bottom. On your way down you will come to where this path joins with a bridlepath coming in on the right. Go straight on (sign to Hound Tor) to the

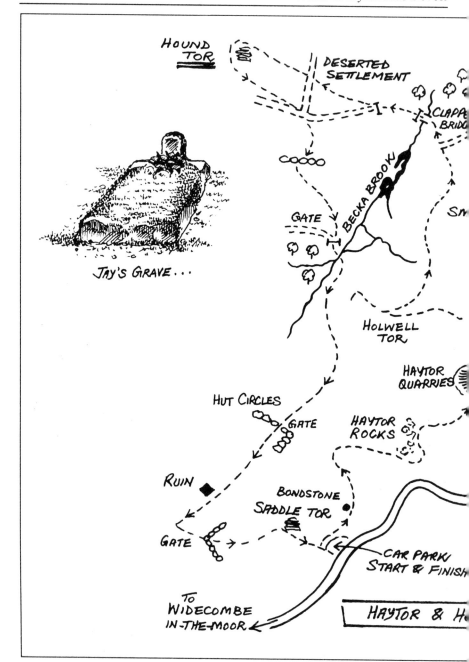

HOUND TOR

DESERTED SETTLEMENT

CLAPP
BRID

BECKA BROOK

GATE

SN

JAY'S GRAVE . . .

HOLWELL TOR

HAYTOR QUARRIES

HUT CIRCLES

GATE

HAYTOR ROCKS

RUIN

BONDSTONE

SADDLE TOR

GATE

CAR PARK
START & FINISH

TO
WIDECOMBE
IN-THE-MOOR

HAYTOR & H

ICOMBE
KS

HAYTOR
DOWN

To BOVEY TRACEY

D TOR

valley bottom woods where a mix of trees including hawthorn, birch, oak and rowan often holds much bird and other wildlife interest. Cross the clapper bridge at Becka Brook and go on up the valley side and through a wooden gate. You will find Greater Rocks at the top of the hill on the left. Walk straight on down to the ancient Hound Tor settlement site, and from the 'village' on to Hound Tor itself.

Another site of sad local interest, Jay's Grove, is below Hound Tor at a point where three parishes meet. Kitty Jay was an 18th-century servant girl and orphan, placed on a farm to work in drudgery. She was, it is said, seduced by her employer and driven out of the parish in disgrace, whereupon, in despair, she hanged herself. To this day fresh flowers are found on her grave, recently placed, and legend has it she is beloved of the pixies of the moor who show her greater compassion than her own folk ever did. Say a prayer for her here. Pixie and fairy song has often been heard here at Hound Tor on Midsummer's Eve.

The stone buildings of this hamlet consist of eight houses, a shed and three drying barns for corn and dating from the mid-13th century. Beneath this hamlet lie turf-walled structures dating to the 7th century. Dowsing suggests that much earlier settlements existed to prehistoric times. Dowsing at a standing stone not far from Hound Tor ages the stone at this site to 4000 years ago, similar dating to some on Exmoor.

Explore Hound Tor if you will, but to

move on, keep the Tor on your left and follow a path half-right which leads to a wider track and a gateway in the wall ahead which has an information board and finger post. Part of the information refers to a bull which is said not to be dangerous so we move on through the said gate, turning left onto a path waymarked Haytor Down. This leads to another path and a wooden gate with a path to the right beneath trees to Becka Brook. Cross this and walk up to a path routed parallel to the valley. Turn right and follow it through bracken for several hundred metres then detour half-left up a stony slope to avoid boggy ground, continuing on and round left and you will have Rippon Tor in view ahead. Make for the enclosure wall which bends in a dog-leg to the left to a gate. Go through the gate (which is marked 'Footpath to Hemsworthy Gate') and continue straight on along the red waymarked route, passing broken walls and field ruins on the right. Take the left turn at the next path junction, waymarked to Saddle Tor, and leave the enclosure via the gate to continue half-left for the summit of Saddle Tor and then the drop down to the car park.

Walk 7: Postbridge to Cranmere Pool and back via Furtor and Cut Hill

Grid Reference: SX 646788

Distance: 15½ miles (25km)

Terrain: Five climbs and some stiles. Not to be taken in bad weather. Strenuous walk.

Refreshments: Postbridge

Starting Point: Postbridge car park

The walk is partly through Okehampton and Merrivale firing ranges so check firing times.

This is Dartmoor's great northern fen, real wild moorland, a walker's walk and not for a family outing with the children unless they are of an age to already be tiring you out on tough rambles. Postbridge's car park on the B3212 is the starting point. Before the road came there was a ford and the medieval clapper bridge, a lovely sight and much photographed these days.

The area is haunted by a huge pair of hairy hands which actually seem malevolent in that two fatalities at least have occurred because of them. Both these cases involved motor cycles, one a man riding alone so it is difficult to blame the hands, but the other incident also involved a pillion passenger who escaped with serious injuries. He said he saw a hairy hand touch the handle-bar and upset the machine. Another incident involved a young male guest at Penlee in Postbridge who, whilst riding his motor cycle to Princetown, felt his hands gripped by two rough and hairy hands, and every effort made to upset the machine.

Tales of the hairy hands go back to horse and carriage days, along with most menacingly powerful feelings of horror and, on occasions, terrifying screams have been reported. Yet another incident involved a family sleeping in a caravan. The mother awoke as her husband and child slept. Seeing a hairy hand rising up the window which was open slightly at the top, she immediately gave the sign

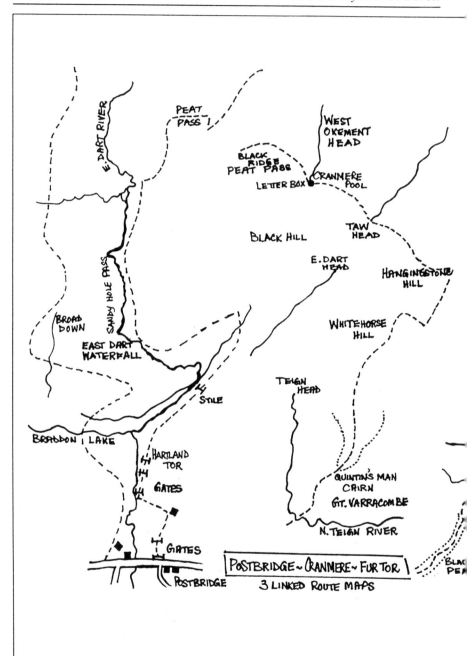

POSTBRIDGE~CRANMERE~FUR TOR
3 LINKED ROUTE MAPS

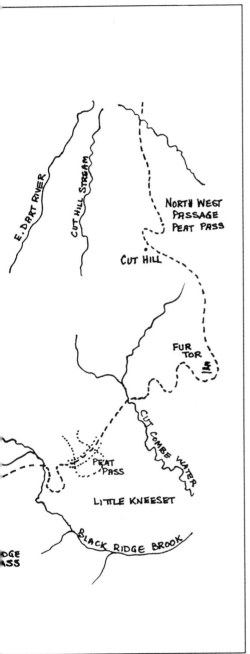

of the cross and began to pray. At this the hand dropped back and the feeling of dread disappeared. This was among the old ruins of the Powder Mills, a deserted gunpowder factory just west of Postbridge and half a mile (800m) to the north of the haunted road. So, be glad you are only walking and not on a motor cycle as we set out.

From the car park go left on the main road, passing the post office and village store on your left, then over the road bridge running parallel to the medieval clapper bridge. Turn left after crossing the bridge and go through the gate next to a five-barred gate, following the wall across the field, right, towards Ringhill. Then go left, following the wall to the river. Go through another gate and turn right, going upstream and through two more gates in the Hartyland plantation.

The path now enters Hartland Tor Newtake and goes up the East Dart Valley close to the riverbank, which passes below the tor. Cross the stile over the stone wall at the far end of the newtake and go into the Stannon Tor Newtake. Go on by the river to where the Lade Hill Bottom tributary stream comes in from the north, and the East Dart swings sharply left. Cross the stream close to where it enters the East Dart above a weir and go on in the same direction on the uphill path. Follow it left, going upstream by the river. Go through the gate, keeping to the path, and cross Winney's Down Brook, following the path round the left side of the hill to the bottom of the waterfall.

Stay on the left bank and go up the valley to Sandy Hill Pass, with considerable tin-stream spoils to your left. Follow the path over the top of the pass with the Broad Marsh valley before you. Go on along the path above the flood plain and straight on to a shallow combe, turning right up the hill to follow the peat pass to a ruined house on Winney's Down called Statts House.

Walk north along the down crest towards the lookout hut and cairn of Quintin's Man, where you pass another peat cutter's home on your left. Go down into the valley of the South Teign river, keeping notice boards and range poles on the left, then cross the river and go on up following the poles. From the lookout hut go straight on along the MOD track, north-east, keeping the range poles well to the right. On Whitehorse Hill follow the granite track right through the peat pass from 240 metres (800ft), then go left and around to Hangingstone Hill Tor. From the observation post go left onto a path towards Taw Head, crossing above a bluff above the source of the River Taw. Avoid the boggy area to the left of Taw Head for this is the source of the East Dart river and can be very treacherous. From the top of the hill you can see the oval-shaped shallow depression of haunted Cranmere Pool itself, where begin the Tavy and Okement rivers. It is also said that the Taw begins here, then travels via Belstone and North Tawton to Barnstaple in North Devon, meeting the lovely Torridge river, which comes off the Okement, at Barnstaple and Bideford Bay.

Cranmere, the cradle of rivers, is bleak and haunted. Here Gayer, former Mayor of Okehampton, baled out the pool with a sieve until he flooded the town and paid penance in a different way (see Okehampton Castle walk). Today he haunts the pool as a black pony or black dwarf. I promise you, on one visit to this spot on a drizzly day in the 70s, when a very dark coloured pony snorted and trotted towards me out of the mist, I was away very quickly from the area. Beyond the pool, which was once an imposing tarn said to be bottomless, lies West Okement Head, and beyond that, Great Links Tor.

You can visit Cranmere Pool and the post-box surrounded by granite slabs – it is a truly wild place, full of atmosphere. Why not sign the visitors' book then move on over the hill. Keep West Okement Head to your right, and halfway up the hill cut across to the peat pass marker and go on up to Black Ridge where stone cairns show the route. Follow the pass, which is just over 1000 metres and head for Fur Tor.

Go on towards Fur Tor, 572 metres ahead, and drop down to Black Ridge Brook, crossing the stream to turn right. Go downstream for 185 metres, picking a dry route to avoid boggy ground. Above the marsh bear left again, following the hillside for about 275 metres to join another peat pass on the right which cuts across the lowest end of Little Kneeset. Walk on to find Fur Tor again in sight over the hill and aim for the left side of it, dropping down to Cut Combe Water. Cross the stream and head for the summit of Fur Tor by keeping on towards the left pile, then going half-right to traverse the hillside. Go past the main pile and straight on, keeping the south bank of Cut Combe Water on your left. Now follow the path and range poles up to Cut Hill.

At Cut Hill turn right at the notice boards and go south towards Hessery Tor radio mast for about 140 metres. On reaching the North-West Passage pass, marked by two stone cairns, turn left and follow the marker cairns downhill. At the end of the pass, go on down along a less well-defined path, keeping the West Dart source well to the right. You will now see two range poles ahead. Aim for the left of these, keeping the valleys of the East Dart and Cut Hill stream on your left.

Now we are on rough terrain over humps and tussocks so go carefully on. Cross the stream over the next hilltop and pass a range pole to cross a gully with spoil heaps, then go on towards a combe with its head on the right. Now a better path runs from the combe over the hilltop. It disappears again, but you continue on in the same direction. You can now see Fernworthy Forest, good for crossbills, and the East Dart waterfall to your left. Go on along the same contour and over Broad Down, passing the dip below the waterfall to climb over the down and head for the clearly visible cairn ahead.

From the cairn go down left over a combe and aim for a granite outcrop to the newtake wall. Follow this to where it turns right and cross the stile to follow the boundary wall left downhill along the public path. Nearing Breddon Lake Bottom the wall goes to the left. Walk straight on over old boundary work, crossing the leat via the clapper bridge, over Breddon Lake Bottom and along the bridlepath. Hartland Tor is on your left, with the Roundy Park Kistvaen lying in an enclosure. Walk along the track called Drift Lane and back to Postbridge car park.

Note: Wistman's Wood (SX 612722) Many readers will want to visit the famous Wistman's Wood whilst on Dartmoor. It lies just south-east of Postbridge, about 1¾ miles along the B3212. It is signed over a clapper bridge to the right of the road and directly east, with Powder Mills Farm to our left and Littaford Tors beyond. The 1½ mile walk from the road is well worthwhile. Wistman's Wood was once much larger, but even today has an eerie presence for many, though I find it a pleasing place. It is thought by some to have Druid connections and dowsing here, one finds a remarkably powerful ley, strengthening at midsummer.

This is an indigenous oak wood, one of only three remaining on the high moors, the others being Piles Wood (644620) and Black Tor Beare (566890). The stunted and weirdly-shaped oaks and rock formations give a magical appearance and feel to Wistman's Wood, where twigs upon the ground may suddenly become adders, and vice versa! Here, too, is a massive boulder recording details of a tree felled in 1866, and some interesting birdlife and other wildlife for such a remote, wooded site of only about 3 hectares. The trees here are Pedunculate oak, whereas in such acidic soils one might have expected to find Sessile oaks. The trees are about 500-years-old and, of course, should be Pedunculate if we bear in mind that the long stalks to the acorn cups make the pipes smoked by pixies! Here, too, are ferns, mosses and lichens in abundance, and an interesting flora to please any visiting nature lover. And, of course, the Wild Hunt. Two of the favourite haunts of the spectral huntsman and his pack of demon Wisht or Yeth Hounds are Wistman's Wood and the Dewerstone Rock, both strange places to be as the sun sets and night begins to fall upon the wild moor.

Walk 8: Pew Tor and Vixen Tor

Grid Reference: SX 531751
Distance: 3½ miles (5km)
Terrain: Wild moorland, mostly level walking.
Refreshments: None
Starting Point: Car park, top of Pork Hill on B3357

Go to the west end of the car park where an information board describes the panoramic view. It was erected to commemorate the 70th anniversary of the Royal Town Planning Institute. Turn left out of the car park and go straight on south to find the well-defined track flanked on the right for a short distance by large boulders. Go over the leat and where the track passes close by a field boundary wall on the right, bear left along a narrow path making for the Windy Post Cross, sometimes called Beckamoor Cross. The converging tracks here link Chagford and Ashburton with Tavistock.

Go over the Grimstone Leat and continue on to Feather Tor which rises to 1028ft (313m) above sea level. Now go straight on to Pew Tor which can be seen in the distance, crossing over the branch leat then keeping this on your left.

Now go left downhill, following an old cart track and keeping the boundary wall on your right and Heckwood Tor on the left. Go by Heckwood Quarry on the left. The large, dressed granite block here, destined for Plymouth's breakwater in 1812, was found to be flawed and thus abandoned. Now you can see Vixen Tor ahead. Strangely enough, when I was there in the spring a female fox was living in a lair beneath the Tor, so yes, Vixen Tor indeed.

Cross the Beckamoor Water via the fording place and go uphill to the stile leading into Vixen Tor Newtake. Go over and straight up the hill, keeping the pile on the right. Vixen Tor is a delightful spot and rightly called the Sphinx of Dartmoor, it is my own favourite place on this moorland. There is a good example of a cist between the tor and the enclosure wall to the north (Kistvaen).

From the tor go left, keeping your back to the Walkham Valley,

Vixen Tor

leaving the newtake by the stile. Go straight on, following Beckamoor Water upstream and keeping the combe on your left. Go to the gulley top, where an aqueduct carries the Grimstone Leat over Beckamoor Water, and bear left over the lower north slope of Barn Hill, crossing over a leat-diverting channel. Head back to the car park, keeping the main road on your right. The leat is about 500-years-old and takes water from the River Walkham below Great Mis Tor and back in again about 7 miles further on.

Pew Tor is 1000ft (305m) above sea level. Although the rock basins are a natural formation, it is possible that the suggested Druidical Seats of Judgement were so used at one time. Vixen Tor, overlooking the River Walkham valley, is the highest tor on Dartmoor. From the ground to its summit is 93ft (29m) on its south face. Tor is from the Celtic *twr*, meaning a tower, so the term is well-used on Dartmoor which has about 170 tors in all.

Our mysterious element here is threefold, at least. During 1995, four of us were approaching Vixen Tor shortly after lunch time on a splendid summer's day when we espied a figure dancing and

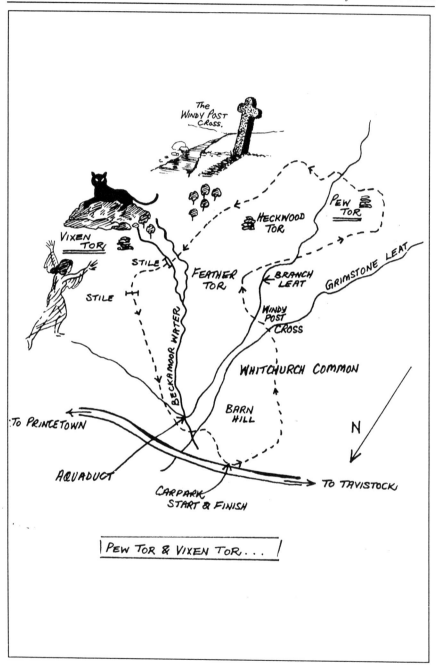

The
WINDY POST
CROSS.

PEW
TOR

HECKWOOD
TOR

VIXEN
TOR

STILE

FEATHER
TOR

BRANCH
LEAT

GRIMSTONE LEAT

STILE

BECKAMOOR WATER

WINDY
POST
CROSS

WHITCHURCH COMMON

N

BARN
HILL

:TO PRINCETOWN

AQUADUCT

CARPARK
START & FINISH

TO TAVISTOCK

| PEW TOR & VIXEN TOR . . . |

whirling gracefully amongst the hawthorns near a standing stone. As we approached closer and I prepared my camera for a photo, we could see it was a women in diaphanous loose clothing which swirled about her. I stopped to focus the camera and could not find her in shot. Then one of my companions said, "She's gone, she just went." Another said she danced behind the smallish standing stone, which is only about 3ft tall, and vanished.

Also in 1995, at about the time reports of a puma came from the Haytor area, we saw one here basking in the sun, about a third of the way up Vixen Tor. It, too, disappeared, but cats can do that. During 1996, a line of three monks was observed by a party of walkers in daylight. Each monk was wearing a brown habit, and they followed each other slowly around the side of the tor, away from the road. One walker told me he left the small party he was with and hurried after them, only to see the last monkish figure crouch to go into a passage beneath the tor. He dashed forward, looked in and there was no one at all inside, even though the end of the rock passage could be seen. The walkers were from Lancashire and not given to fantasies or flights of imagination of this kind. So, enjoy this walk and have that camera at the ready.

Walk 9: Lustleigh Cleave Circular Walk

Grid Reference: SX 784793

Distance: 7 miles (11km)

Terrain: Not difficult – 3 short climbs, all public paths.

Refreshments: None

Starting Point: Trendlebere Down car park

This is a beautiful, wooded river walk in an area where fairies are reported to have been seen as recently as the 1990s. The little people were dressed in browns and greens and the most recent sighting passed to me was made by a mother and her two youngsters who live near Newton Abbot.

This is one of the fire-devastated areas of Dartmoor which, thankfully, began greening over rapidly as soon as the rains came. It was, however, a disaster for wildlife and a sombre warning to be extremely careful during dry conditions. Even a bottle left lying about can act as a lens to direct the sun's concentrated rays and start a fire, with matches and cooking (camping) fires being even worse hazards.

From the car park go down the track along the woodland edge on the right. This is the Old Manaton Road, now unsuitable for vehicular use. Carry on where the track levels and goes by part of the National Nature Reserve, continuing along the track amongst the trees. Ignore a path on the right and go straight on to the Becka Brook. Cross over the footbridge on the right. Turn right and follow the path which goes left as it follows round the wooded Houndtor Ridge.

We are now in the Bovey valley. Go upstream with the river on your right for about 1 mile, and at the footbridge of tree-trunks and handrail cross over the river. Follow the path up the side of the cleave signed 'Lustleigh', and on reaching the junction, continue straight up the slope ignoring the right turn. Now a short, steep climb leads to another junction where you turn left, signed ' Foxworthy Bridge', and go down the hill, keeping Sharpitor Rocks on your right.

Near the valley bottom a path leads left signed 'Horsham for

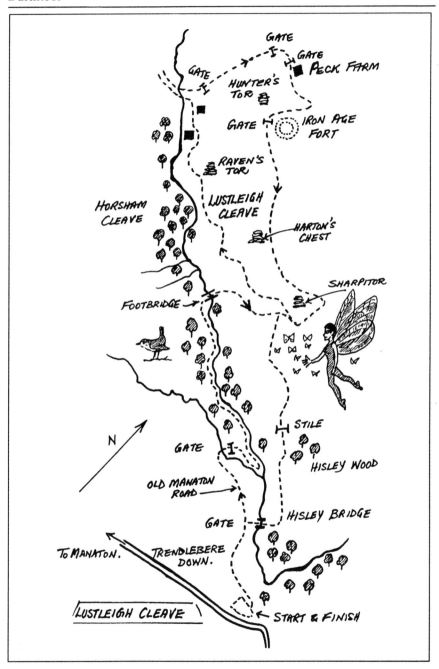

GATE

GATE

GATE PECK FARM

HUNTER'S TOR

GATE

GATE IRON AGE FORT

RAVEN'S TOR

LUSTLEIGH CLEAVE

HORSHAM CLEAVE

HARTON'S CHEST

SHARPITOR

FOOTBRIDGE

N

STILE

GATE

HISLEY WOOD

OLD MANATON ROAD

GATE HISLEY BRIDGE

TO MANATON.

TRENDLEBERE DOWN.

LUSTLEIGH CLEAVE

START & FINISH

Manaton and Water'. Continue on along the path to Foxworthy, passing the mill on the left. At Foxworthy Bridge go right to follow the track signed 'Peck Farm and Road near Barnecourt'. This goes left in front of houses at Foxworthy. Go through the gate, turn right and go up to Peck Farm. Keeping the farmhouse on the left, go through a gate and up the side of the field, going left again at the top to follow the path which swings back right to Hunter's Tor.

At Hunter's Tor, go through the gate where you will see the low ramparts of an Iron Age fort on the left. Continue on along the ridge, passing the outcrops of Harton Chest below on the right, to Sharpitor. Keep to the path beside the wall (left) and go down through the wood keeping the tor to your right, ignoring the path leading to a stile on the left. Near the bottom of the hill, by a gate, go right, signed 'Clam Bridge, Horsham Steps, Heaven's Gate and Lustleigh'. Sharpitor Rocks is again in view, so go along the lower path on the left and down to the next path junction we met earlier. Go straight down the hill to the next path junction and go left, signed 'Lustleigh via Pethybridge' and go straight on. At the path fork, go right for Hisley Bridge and after a short distance go over the stile, into the wood, and continue on down to the river. Now turn right and go over the arched packhorse bridge. Go through the gate, turn left, signed 'Nr. Holne Brake' and continue up the old Manaton road to the starting point.

Note: Lustleigh keeps up its maypole dancing tradition on the first Saturday in May. The town orchard was given to the parish as a permanent site for the May Day Festival.

Walk 10: Norsworthy Bridge, Eylesbarrow, Ditsworthy Warren and Sheepstor

Grid Reference:	SX 568693
Distance:	7½ miles (12km)
Terrain:	3 climbs, wild moorland but a great walk.
Refreshments:	None
Starting Point:	Norsworthy Bridge, north-east end of Burrator Reservoir. Ample car parking beyond the bridge, each side of the road.

You will encounter some wonderful scenery on this walk, perhaps some of the best on Dartmoor. Norsworthy Bridge spans the River Meary. On the left, go along the road towards Sheepstor, over a roadbridge crossing Narrator Brook. In a few paces the road goes half-right. Leave the road here and go straight on along the walled lane with forestry on the right. Pass what is left of Middleworth Farm on the right, and Middleworth Tor can be seen above the trees on your left. When you reach the farm settlement ruins at Deancombe, pass the first group of buildings and before reaching the more modern (19th-century) remains, go left up a tree-lined path next to an old mining adit. Pass a sheep pen and go through the gate ahead leading onto the open moor. Go straight up for a short distance to bear half-left towards the summit of Down Tor.

A stone alignment, known as the Down Tor Row, runs from a retaining circle about 650 metres east-south-east of the tor, terminating about 200 metres short of a cairn on the same line. A ley runs along the stone row which dowses at its most active in summer.

From Down Tor go right through the clitter field on the east slope to find a path running parallel with and to the left of the stone-walled enclosure. Go uphill to where the wall goes right and go on half-left to the crest of this hill. Cross the boundary work, which is a prehistoric reave or parallel boundary system dated by dowsing to some 4000 years old. The reason for this method of boundary

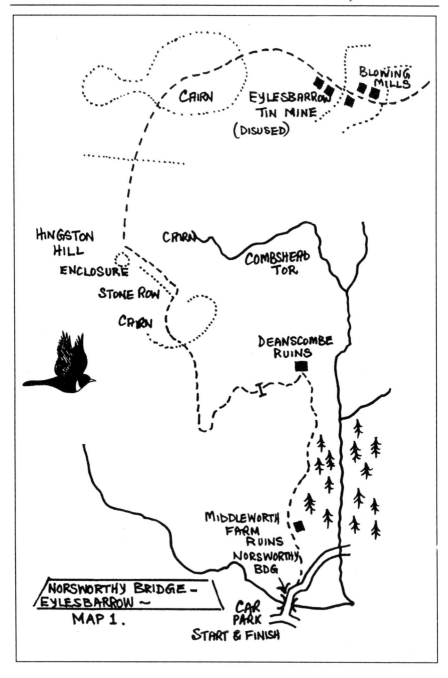

BLOWING MILLS

CAIRN   EYLESBARROW
                     TIN MINE
                     (DISUSED)

HINGSTON
HILL   CAIRN
ENCLOSURE   COMBSHEAD
                                          TOR
STONE ROW

CAIRN
                                 DEANSCOMBE
                                   RUINS

                          MIDDLEWORTH
                             FARM
                             RUINS
                          NORSWORTHY
                             BDG

NORSWORTHY BRIDGE –
EYLESBARROW –
   MAP 1.   CAR
                              PARK
                         START & FINISH

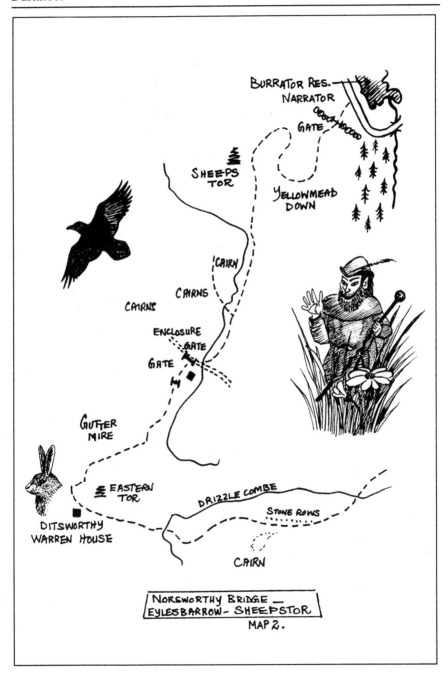

NORSWORTHY BRIDGE —
EYLESBARROW— SHEEPSTOR
MAP 2.

marking remains unsolved by archaeologists, but where it occurs there is usually a ley along the route, the importance of which is yet to be acknowledged by science.

Now head for the single stone row and circle on the level plain of Hingston Hills, following the row to the furthest end to go on half-left to a circular enclosure then on to the cairn, a huge pile of stones. Go straight on with the tinners' gullies on your right and at the head of these go half-right to go uphill to the summit of Eylesbarrow.

At the bondstone between two cairns, go straight along the path down to the ruins of Eylesbarrow tin mine and towards the china clay spoil heaps. As you get close bear half-left for the furthest building. Be warned, exploring old mine workings can be very dangerous, best to adhere to the walk route. Turn right onto the track and go down past old blowing mill foundations and, on the right, a row of granite flat-rod supports for transmitting power. Carry on the track past an old wall on the left, and after about 200 metres another track goes half-left. Go along this and down to the ruin of a smelting house, then on to the ford over Drizzlecombe to go round to the right towards Shavercombe Tor.

Now make for the Drizzlecombe stone rows and the huge Giant's Basin cairn to follow these down to the last menhir, heading for Scots pine trees on the horizon to the left of Eastern Tor to find a track leading to Ditsworthy Warren. Pass the house on the left at Ditsworthy Warren and bear right to follow Edward's Path around the lower part of Eastern Tor. On reaching the Scots pines, go through the gate by the Scouts' hut on the right then through another gate to turn right onto the track for some 140 metres. Cross the leat, go left and follow the line of the waterway, keeping the leat on the left until two bondstones are reached. Cross the leat and go straight on to Yellowmead Stone Circle, an interesting multiple circle. There is evidence of an associated double row of stones here.

Go back to the bondstones, cross the leat and bear left to follow its route uphill to where it swings sharply left, going half-left to the summit of Sheepstor. Now we are at a magical place, indeed, a lonely, beautiful spot with the pixies' castle or cave, a rocky cavern with a seat in it. I met with a women here who said she had seen pixies at Sheepstor and that they showed her how to make a powerful drink with honey and herbs which, "puts me and my 'usband fair silly and then us sleeps it off."

As to the pixie castle, some books suggest it is a cavern beneath Sheepstor, as if you can simply find it at ground level. Not so, the climb to it is considerable and could be dangerous so I suggest you enjoy the wonderful tor as it is, a most majestic sight, and leave its mystery and the pixies to their own devices. Better to be safe than sorry.

It is in this same cavern that the Royalist, Elford, hid from Cromwell's troops, an excellent vantage point commanding views over the moorland. Evidently he passed the time by painting the interior walls and Mrs. Bray's *Traditions of Devonshire* makes mention of this and of someone who saw the wall paintings. Alas, they are no longer there, or I should say, fortunately, as I prefer the site in its natural state.

Now follow the summit ridge north (left) then bear right down the slope. About halfway down, go left towards Narrator Plantation.

Burrator

Follow the wall to the left to a small hunting-gate going through where, on the right, are the Narrator Farm ruins, one of the farms lost following the building of Burrator reservoir. Go along the bridlepath half-left between two granite gateposts and on reaching the road, go right for about 800 metres to Norsworthy Bridge.

Note: Eylesbarrow is 1490ft (454m) above sea level. Drizzlecombe stone rows date to over 4500 years when dowsed, the Giant's Basin dating about the same. It is 21 metres in diameter. Ditsworthy Warren is a purpose-built rabbit warren, probably from Norman Conquest times, and the rabbits were used as food. It was eventually built to cover 445 hectares (1100 acres) and was Dartmoor's largest. If you discover a pixie's home and disturb it, you should leave a pin or some other offering for good luck. I know someone who will be reading this book who chuckled when I told him this at Sheepstor, saying I was being silly. I left an offering of three linked safety pins, as is my wont. He fell the last third or so of the climb back down from the tor and was quite shaken and bruised.

Exmoor

Exmoor is the softer of the two Devon moors, but, like Dartmoor, is a national park. About a third of Exmoor lies in Devon, the remainder in Somerset, and our walks occasionally take us over the county border, albeit briefly.

Although Exmoor is known for its purple heather moors and red deer country, a great deal of it is farmed, mainly for sheep and cattle. There is also the Exmoor coastline and coastal habitats with rugged cliffs and splendid sea views across to Wales. For the best of the purple heather visit from August into the autumn. September and October are the months for the red deer rut.

This is the land of the Doones where mysterious tales and legends include those of King Arthur, and where ghosts and hauntings are very much a part of the region's fascination. Remember, too, the Beast of Exmoor – a composite animal really, based on pumas, leopards and even wolverines and werewolves. Happy walking.

Walk 11: Valley of Rocks to Woody Bay and Hunter's Inn, Heddon Valley

Grid Reference: SS 705495 (Valley of Rocks) or SS 680490 (Woody Bay)

Distance: 8 miles (11km)

Terrain: Well-maintained (NT) coastal path, some steep ascents on return walk from Hunter's Inn

Refreshments: Hunter's Inn

Starting Point: Valley of Rocks car park

This can be a short or long circular walk to suit the time available. The walking is mainly on footpaths, but there is some road-walking. The car park at Valley of the Rocks is reached at the west end of Lee Road, Lynton.

Where better to begin a walk than from the delightful Valley of the Rocks with its magnificent scenery and sea views. The walker

Valley of Rocks

will be immediately struck (figuratively speaking) by the weird and wonderful rock formations that give the valley its name. It would have been scenically even more impressive a couple of centuries ago as a great stone circle once stood here, with both Bronze Age and Druidic connections, but soon after 1850 it was destroyed by vandals. However, nothing can destroy the spirit of the place as the walker will soon discover.

Walk into the valley along the road, away from Lynton, with the amazing rock formations of Ragged Jack and Castle Rock on your right, the Devil's Cheesewring on your left. Ragged Jack, some say Ragged Dick, was said to be a local character caught by the devil dancing with several of his friends on a Sunday. They were turned into slate, and there they remain.

Signed to the Devil's Cheesewring is Mother Meldrum's Kitchen. Her ghost is sometimes said to be seen here on moonlit nights. Mother Meldrum, the wise woman of R.D. Blackmore's *Lorna Doone*, the healer and soothsayer whom Jan Ridd went to seek advice from when he fell in love with Lorna. A wise woman, Aggie Norman, actually did live here in the Valley of Rocks, where once a river ran where the road now is. Look for the herd of wild goats here. They live in the valley and may often be seen browsing amongst the bracken and gorse-clad slopes, quite used to visitors and a truly feral herd, living and breeding in the wild.

On up the road, past the viewing point to the White Lady, we come to Lee Abbey, an imposing building which never was an abbey but originally built as a dwelling. Today it is the home of an Anglican lay community. It was built on the site of the manor where the De Wichehalse family once lived.

On the seaward clifftop you will see the tower of Duty Point, believed to be the very tower depicted by the great English landscape artist Samuel Palmer (1805-1881) who painted here during his visits to the West Country. See his painting and etchings of 'The Lonely Tower' made in the 1860s and 70s. It is interesting, too, that Palmer referred to "those so-called Druidic stones" in a letter at that time to L.R. Valpy, solicitor to John Ruskin.

The Duty Point tower overlooks an area today known as Jenny's

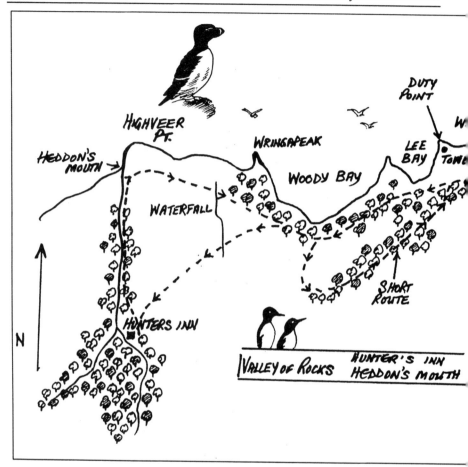

Leap where rugged cliffs break the force of the sea waves dashing against the jagged rocks below. 'Jenny' was Jennifried De Wichehalse, the beautiful heiress to the house, only daughter of her widowed father and betrothed to a nobleman in high favour at the court of Charles I. On the morning of their wedding a messenger brought news that her lover had deserted her and was married to another. That night she wandered from her home and her lifeless body was found on the rocks at the base of the cliffs forming the promontory of Duty Point next day.

Any justice was denied her father but strangely, in 1643, De

CLIFF

VALLEY OF ROCKS
START + FINISH

MOTHER MELDRUM.

Wichehalse and Lord Auberly, the betrayer of his daughter, were on opposing sides in the Battle of Lansdown, near Bath. Auberly was killed by De Wichehalse, but a year later the King's troops invaded the Valley of Rocks and drove the Wichehalses from their home. They put to sea in a barque, but bodies were found on the beach from the wreck of the little boat and De Wichehalse himself, though not found, was never heard of again. Walk here then on fine, sunny days but do come here if you can on a moonlit night to let these tales wash over you where they really happened. Magic.

But on we must go down the steep road to the toll house, fee for vehicles, and on past the charming tea rooms and Lee Bay. Follow the road up under shady trees with hanging oakwoods reaching down to the sea, to a wooden gateway overlooking Woody Bay and superb views. On the left-hand side of the road is a lay-by with a wooden gate. If you have chosen the short walk this is your way back, a delightfully shady, wooded walk, well-waymarked, which brings you out eventually on to the road by Lee Abbey entrance once again, so an easy walk back to the Valley of Rocks.

The longer walk takes us on up to Woody Bay car park (you can begin here if you like) where, just a way up from a wooden seat at the roadside we find kissing gates leading off the road and along an excellent pathway, away from all vehicles and cycles.This is a joy of a walk following a curving pathway with fine sea views and much wildlife including razorbills and guillemots which nest on the rugged cliffs. Try it on a summer's evening as the setting sun bathes everything in a golden light, all the way to the historic Hunter's Inn where food and drink can be had. Just up the road is a National Trust shop should you want to take home a memento of your journey, or maybe purchase an OS map.

From the exit path beside the inn, retrace your footsteps for a short distance to find a waymarked and signed path on the left (to Heddon's Mouth). Follow the waymarked route which gradually wends its steep way up over the cliff face, providing stunning views of the Heddon Cleave, the river and, by the beach, the old lime kiln, scene of Tarka the Otter's short stay here during the Williamson story. Keep on going up, and up, to where the path goes east and, thankfully, downhill until you turn a corner right to see the lovely Hollowbrook Waterfall ahead. Fine photo opportunities here and sightings of razorbills and guillemots skimming the waves or enjoying the bathing. Carry on along the path, over a stile, and on to a gate leading on to a tarmac road. Go up the road to the right, passing a house with high, scree-type banks retained by wire mesh, and on to the main road, turning right to find your way uphill to the starting point car park for some. Alternatively, carry on left down the hill to Woody Bay Hotel on your right, and back on down to find the road to the Valley of the Rocks.

Walk 12: Tarr Steps from Dulverton and back

Grid Reference: SX 868322

Distance: 10 miles (16km)

Terrain: Fairly easy, some good paths.

Refreshments: Dulverton

Starting Point: Dulverton

If you can manage a walk of more than 10 miles, then do try this one. This is Lorna Doone country so – you must choose an inn in the old town and have a hot pasty to savour the comfort found by Jan Ridd and John Fry after Ridd's father had been killed by the Doones. Yes, we are still in Doone country and who knows where you may see or feel the spirit of Lorna on these walks. The young daughter of the Countess Dugal is ever about the wilds of Exmoor one feels.

Follow the road up out of the town along the lovely Barle river,

Tarr Steps

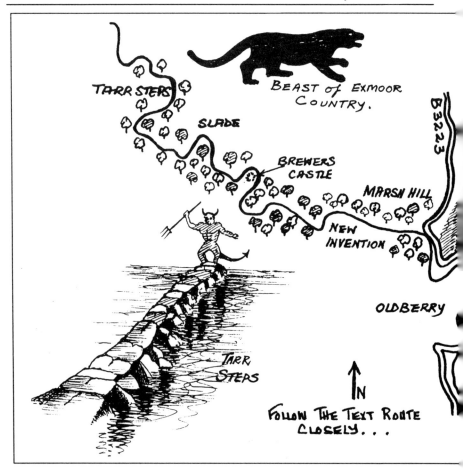

TARR STEPS

BEAST of EXMOOR COUNTRY.

SLADE

B3223

BREWERS CASTLE

MARSH HILL

NEW INVENTION

OLDBERRY

TARR STEPS

↑N

FOLLOW THE TEXT ROUTE CLOSELY. . .

with the church above you on the right. Walk for about a half mile between wooded hills to a stout bridge over the Barle. To your left is Northmoor church with a cottage nearby. Here a path leads down to the river, an old route used by anglers. Do not cross the bridge, but instead follow the lane over Winsford Hill with views of the Barle on the left for a while. Soon you are faced with open expanses of Exmoor, and about 3 miles beyond Northmoor church we follow right to the signposted Caractacus Stone, inscribed in the Dark Ages as they are so wrongly called. The inscription reads CARAACI NEPVS, possibly 'Kinsman of Caractacus'.

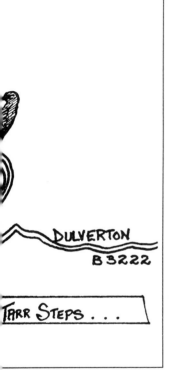

Now take the left-hand route. Tarr Steps is but a mile and a half ahead and we are once more in wooded country. Head past a farm and downhill to where the Barle awaits us, shallow here and broad in summer, wild when in flood conditions. Now you can view Tarr Steps clapper bridge in all its glory. Even today no one knows its date of origin or who built it, though folklore and legend say it was the devil's work. If it was, he had an eye for beauty. I've dowsed here and invariably date to 3500 years, or near enough, with the same dowsing results in the 1990s as in the 70s so it's an old bridge site, indeed.

Mother Meldrum's summer home was here according to legend and is referred to in *Lorna Doone*. Personally, I would have wintered here and summered in the Valley of Rocks, but she knew what she was about. Tarr Steps has a total length of about 60 metres, with some of the stone slabs, the steps, weighing up to two tons each. For Beast of Exmoor enthusiasts, both lynx and black panthers have been seen hereabouts in recent years. Yes, truly. (see Further Reading)

Cross the steps and follow the lower path, then at the next bend, the Hawkridge Road. Next follow the waymarked footpath down to the riverside and back to Northmoor. The Exmoor National Park Authority see that routes are well looked after and signposted. Hold to waymarked routes and you will have no problems.

Dulverton is a sizeable town with all the facilities you may need including shops with food, films for cameras and such. The Exmoor National Park Authority Headquarters are here at Dulverton House, a fitting home in what is a thriving rural centre in delightful countryside.

Walk 13: Wood Barrow, the Longstone Menhir and back via Challacombe

Grid Reference: SS 716411

Distance: 5½ miles (9km)

Terrain: Tough, often wet moorland with some long, steady ascents and ill-defined paths.

Refreshments: At Challacombe village (SS 694412)

Starting Point: Breakneck Hole car park (SS 716411)

This is a fine walk, not for softies yet not overlong and after all, you can take as long as you wish. Expect mud on your boots, but there

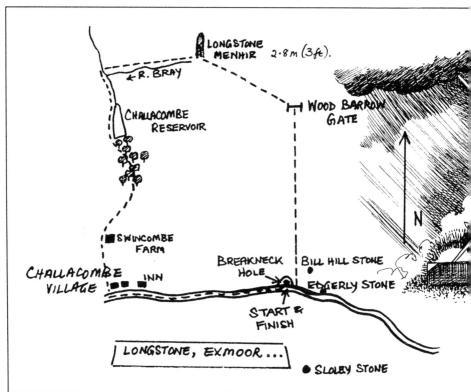

is such a mix of habitats and splendid views that you will hardly notice. A diversion to Pinkworthy (Pinkery) Pond is possible.

Walk up the road away from Challacombe and in a 100 metres or so you will come to a very wide gateway with a stile on the left side of the road. At the beginning of this walk you will find the Bill Hill and Edgerley standing stones on an interestingly powerful ley situation. They are smallish stones and easily missed so look carefully about you. The path here is not too well defined so walk north following the line of the stone wall to your left. You will be heading uphill on what is a steady upward slope for just less than a mile, to a gate known as Wood Barrow Gate. Just through the gate to your left is Wood Barrow itself.

Legend has it that a magician or wise man divined that there was a brass container of treasure in the barrow and he collected together

a group of local men to help him find the spoils. When they neared the centre of the barrow as it was being dug open, a faintness stole over the group but they continued to dig. Suddenly there was a clap of thunder and the flash of lightning struck deep into the heart of the barrow. When the group recovered they saw a brass pan, green and corroded save where the lightning had struck it. There was a shining spot in the bottom of the otherwise empty pan showing where the wise man had seen the treasure moments before. We can only assume the spirits that guard the barrow saw to it that the treasure was not taken away by the wrong souls.

At Wood Barrow Gate signposts tell you the way to the Longstone and to Pinkworthy Pond, pronounced "pinkery" locally. The pond is but a mile south-east of here and well worth a visit if we are to maintain that mysterious element within our walks. We can soon be back at Wood Barrow to continue our walk to the Longstone, and beyond to Challacombe. Or indeed, if you fall in love with Pinkery, stay and enjoy its atmosphere then take the track due south to the road gate just above Breakneck Hole and your car, your 'starting gate' as it were.

Pinkworthy Pond (723423) is man-made, and was supervised by one John Knight of Simonsbath Lodge. The Knight family came to Exmoor from Worcestershire in 1818, with John recorded as being in sole possession of the Exmoor Forest within a short time of the family's arrival. But we are more interested in the ghost which haunts the pond, that of a young farmer who drowned there in 1880, his hat and coat found upon the bank. No amount of dragging found the body so the ancient device of floating a lit candle on a loaf of bread was tried. However, the Exmoor winds did not permit the candle to be lit and the loaf did not come to rest over the body. Divers were brought in from Cardiff to no avail so the pond was drained and the body found close to the bank in shallow water.

The Longstone

The pond is said by many to be a melancholy place. It is true that on a grey, rainy day the atmosphere can be somewhat awesome, but with its surrounding whortleberries and heathers it is a lovely if lonely spot, providing good photography and, if you seek it, moorland solitude.

On from Wood Barrow, Longstone Barrow is in view to the north-west, with the Longstone Menhir just beyond. A path of sorts leads to this wonderful 3 metre tall menhir, the most impressive standing stone on Exmoor. The slate menhir is 75cms at its greatest breadth, though not thicker than 18cms, with its widest face in the north-east and south-west plane. It is a wonderful stone.

From the Longstone, face due south and walk through the high grasses (which may be boggy) and down into a beautiful, narrow combe which takes the narrow, sparkling River Bray almost due west to Swincombe. This is Exmoor at its loveliest, I feel, a narrow, peaceful combe where the Bray is soon joined by the Radworthy Water. This we follow southwards below Swincombe Rocks, or Pixie Rocks as they are locally known. Amongst beech trees here we will find the foundations of an ancient farmhouse, a good place to sit and listen for ring ouzels and perhaps see a fox or wild red deer – not uncommon even in broad daylight.

From here follow the track to Challacombe Reservoir, a secluded, delightful spot where swallows and martins dip over the still waters in spring and summertime, as kestrels and buzzards hover and soar in hunting flight.Go through the gate and under the shady trees of a small wood, then out onto an open farm track with extensive views of cattle and sheep pasture. Pass by the farmstead on the way to the B3358, which we follow east to Challacombe village with its post office shop for refreshments, or the aforesaid Black Venus. Breakneck Hole is further east along this same road.

Walk 14: Countisbury to County Gate (circular)

Grid Reference: SS 747496

Distance: 8 miles (13km)

Terrain: Easy but high ground (1550ft)

Refreshments: None on route

Starting Point: Car park at Countisbury

Go out of the car park by the upper wall gate, and turn left into the churchyard. Go round the west end of the church and out of the churchyard by the stile in the north wall. You emerge onto open cliff top. Walk half-right for 91 metres to a footpath sign and go uphill to the mast and building on the summit of Butter Hill. Walk north to the fenced wall you will see on the right. Here the path steepens to the coast path at a cordoned-off landslide named Great Red. Continue north for 137 metres and take the right turn along the coast path as the true path can be risky to follow. Walk down the steep valley with its scree slopes to the lighthouse path. Turn right up the straight road and bear left at the first hairpin bend along a track signed 'Coast Path'. Pass over the stile by a gate to the remote cottage, and climb a few steps to the coast path. There is a NT sign for Glenthorne Cliffs, and the path enters pleasant mixed woodland with good birdlife and wildflowers. You will now walk via several small combes with their small but lovely waterways, a delightful wooded area with signs of tree pollarding of years gone by. Naturalists should look here for a large tree which has a large boulder in its grips. It is on the higher side of the path, 135 metres west of Pudleep Girt.

About 185 metres east of the Girt, take the safe bypass signposted away from cliff falls uphill, past the ruined folly on the right. The path now levels out, descending back onto the true path then looping around Dogsworthy Combe and Wingate Combe. After Wingate Combe you will come to a fork signed 'Culbone, County Gate'. Take the higher path, looking out for seats and a shelter, then 90 metres on, a stone seat and stone wall with another stone seat. The path now meets Glenthorne Drive so turn right, signed Culbone, and walk by The Lodge, passing the gateposts with their twin boars' heads. On the left you will reach two gates, signed Culbone. Go through the gates, past the Sisters' Fountain and climb 9 metres to an estate drive. Turn right, signed County Gate, and 90 metres beyond turn

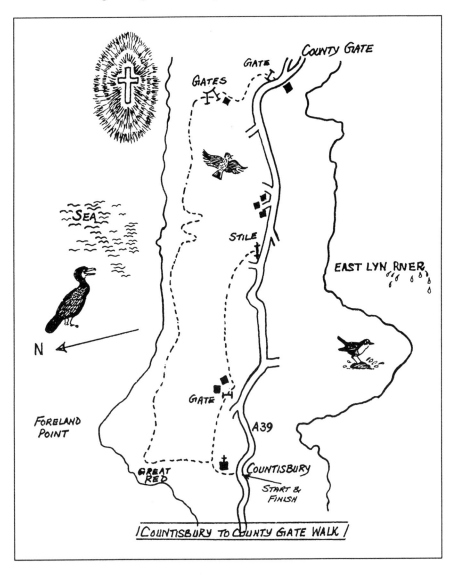

COUNTY GATE
GATE
GATES
SEA
STILE
EAST LYN RIVER
N
FORELAND POINT
GATE
A39
GREAT RED
COUNTISBURY
START & FINISH
/ COUNTISBURY TO COUNTY GATE WALK /

left at Seven Thorns, again signed County Gate. The climb to the A39 is steep.

It is at the beach at Glenthorne, here by County Gate, that it is said that the young Jesus Christ and Joseph of Arimathea beached their ship on the way to Glastonbury. The story goes that they went in search of fresh water and, finding none, Christ caused a spring to rise which has never failed since. Well, that's the story!

Once on the main road, follow it for 9 metres then cross the road to the viewpoint car park at County Gate and the border of Devon with Somerset. At the west end of the car park follow the path over Cosgate Hill. Go down the west side of the hill to a small car park with views of the top end of Glenthorne Drive with its letter-box. From this hillside you can also see the Old Burrow Roman fortlet in the field beyond. Now follow the grass verge on the south side of the A39 for three-quarters of a mile to the stile on the north side of Dogsworthy Cottage. The path crosses fields, is signed for Countisbury and waymarked in yellow. Keeping the field wall on your right, make for the fence in the far corner, going through the gate and keeping the wall right. Pass the gate marked 'To Desolate'. The next gate is 27 metres away from the wall. Now cross the field aiming for the Butter Hill mast in the distance, where you will find a stile.

Walk some 46 metres to a gate waymarked yellow and enter, following the lower edge of the field to another waymarked gate. Go past the round-roofed barn and across the farm road, following the hedge to a gate on the lighthouse road. Cross over and follow the track, taking a left fork after 23 metres then keeping to the main track. Bear left to a footpath sign by the wall. Keep the wall on your left back to Countisbury.

Note: The Foreland is Devon's northernmost point. The lighthouse was built in 1900. The Sisters' Fountain is named after the four sisters, nieces of the Rev W. Halliday who built Glenthorne house in 1832. The drive to Glenthorne House is 3 miles long and drops 288 metres (950ft). Old Burrow (not Old Barrow) is a Roman fortlet which was occupied between AD48 and 52. Probably of little use due to frequent sea mists, it is thought to have been succeeded by the one near Martinhoe between Woody Bay and Heddon's Mouth.

Walk 15: The Doone Valley and Brendon Common, Exmoor

Grid Reference: SS 793477

Distance: 5 miles (8km)

Terrain: Steep moorland in places. Track not distinct so take a compass and avoid bad weather.

Refreshments: Malmsmead, and later Cloud Farm

Starting Point: Malmsmead

Strangely, just as I was about to write this section of the book, I met a couple who had seen a line of 'wild-looking' riders on horseback by the Badgery (Badgworthy) Water in the summer of 1996. The riders, seven of them, six men and a woman who was fourth in the line, rode along the track by the river near Malmsmead dressed in what the couple described as old-fashioned dress. The men wore leather tunics, cloaks and long boots. They were grim-faced and long-haired. The woman was dark-haired and in a long pale dress with a cloak. She, too, looked stern and was about 25-years-old.

The couple told me they realised there was little space as the riders came closer along the riverbank, so they stood back out of the way on a bend, waiting for the first horseman to pass. There was no sound except that of the river and the slight drizzle sweeping down across the combe. When the first horse did not appear the man went to peer round the bend and there were no riders in sight. He called his wife and they rounded the bend to find no one, nor any track leading elsewhere up the steep hillside.

"Even if they'd gone off the track and up the hill we would have still seen them," the man said and his wife agreed. "Anyway, it was straight up, a daft place to go but all those horses could not have got up there so quickly. We waited only 15 seconds as the first horse was virtually on us or we wouldn't have got out of the way. And if they'd gone back we would still have seen them going the other way," he continued.

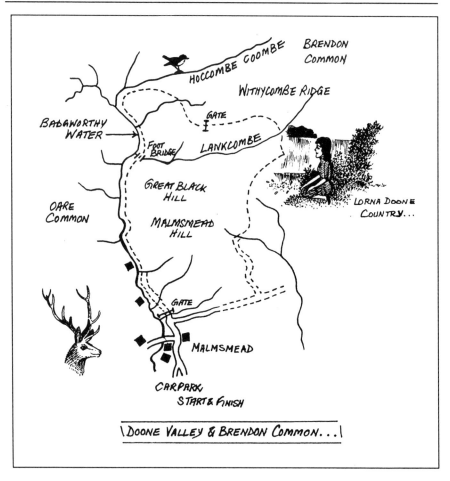

\DOONE VALLEY & BRENDON COMMON...\

"Oh yes. We saw them coming, we'd have seen them leaving, but there's nowhere there to turn seven horses round. And uphill was next to sheer," the woman said. The two were convinced the seven riders had vanished. Vanished into thin air that is. They thought they had seen the Doones, and who was I to suggest they had not? Others have before them and the Doones were real enough once, as were all such strange phenomena – real enough once.

There is a large car park at Malmsmead, a tiny hamlet and a pretty one, with a Lorna Doone Farm Shop and ample refreshments on site. Across the ford with its pretty bridge and just up the hill you will

Malmsmead bridge

find the Field Centre of the Exmoor Natural History Society, though that is not the way we are going. There are dippers here, and wagtails, with many house martins nesting on the eaves of the buildings and swallows zooming everywhere. And this is also red deer country.

Leave the car park and go uphill, south, along the lane signed 'Fullinscott, Slocombeslade and Tippacott'. Where the lane bears right, go through the gate on the left and along the track signed to Doone Valley. The path passes some tall ash trees to the left and weaves about southwards along a waymarked route to drop to Badgery Water with Cloud Farm visible across the river.

Continue on by the river, now more rocky, to the right. Pass the Blackmore memorial stone and go on to Yealscombe and the lovely Badgery Woods. The woods are of oak and ash and support much birdlife including wood warblers.

Cross the stream flowing down Lank Combe via the footbridge in a delightful combe in open woodland. Continue along a steep hillside, crossing Withycombe Ridge Water and finding superb views to the south. The moorland here is known as Deer Park. Follow the path to the foot of Hoccombe Combe where a beech hedgerow crosses in front of you. Now turn away from Badgery Water and follow the well-used track north-west. It passes a medieval village to climb by a ruined cottage then goes down to cross Withycombe Ridge Water. It ascends again to a gate in a wall. Now the track is less well-defined, crossing the rather featureless Withycombe Ridge itself, part of Brendon Common. Head for the prominent signpost to the north on the skyline and follow the track signed 'Malmsmead'. About half a mile on you will come to the meeting place of three tracks. Take the left track, then shortly after go left again, crossing another ford as the track leads to the road about half a mile ahead. Turn right down Post Lane and head back to Malmsmead, about 530 metres away.

Note: The medieval village site is said to be the old Doone settlement, the cottage nearby being much later in date. Present historians tend to argue against the Doones living here, but this is the old Doone site and dowsing here, if you know just what dowsing can achieve, says it is. Do not be deterred by the fact that Blackmore's *Lorna Doone* is a work of fiction. That has never meant that characters, events and places are not based on facts, merely that a writer has built a likely story around them, not having been there to witness them at the time. There are far stranger stories than *Lorna Doone* here on Exmoor.

Beyond Exmoor and Dartmoor

Away from the two moors there are numerous fine walks in Devon. The following have been chosen for their variety and, of course, their mysterious element, as well as for their spread across the county. They should provide the walker with happy times at all points of the compass.There are walks here for all, hardy ramblers and less hardy ramblers. Sounds like a rose garden!

Lundy, Isle of Puffins

Just a few miles off the coast of North Devon lies the island of Lundy. You must never say, "Lundy Island" for "lundy" means "the Puffin Island". Do visit if you can. From Bideford or Ilfracombe there are regular trips to the island that has held its own kingdom, a Christian hermitage, pirates, the retreat of a king, a convict settlement, a royalist stronghold and Turkish seafarers, to name but a few.

Today Lundy is a bird sanctuary, a marine nature reserve and a popular tourist attraction. Even the Marisco Tavern is named from the de Mariscos, ruffians of the 12th century who claimed sovereign powers. Yet they were

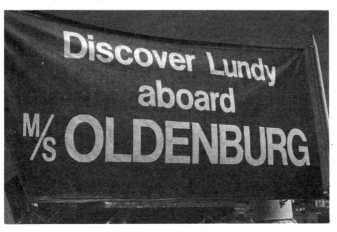

much later than Neolithic man using primitive tools thousands of years ago – some of the tools are found here even now. As far as walking goes this is a sort of free day, for you can wander around the island to your heart's content and meet the true and historic inhabitants of Lundy, the seabirds, and perhaps the occasional rarities, the vagrant species who find landfall here, attracting twitchers from all over the country.

During its early history the islands piratical owners preyed upon Bristol-bound ships, and freebooting continued into the 19th century. Convicts sent to the colonies often got no further than Lundy. One Thomas Benson obtained the government contract to ship convicts abroad, but instead kept some as slaves on the island, where one task was to build him a large house.

Lundy is haunted by a young woman often reported by lighthouse keepers, seen walking the edges of the cliffs. She is thought to be a widow who threw herself over after her husband's death.

Lundy is today a Landmark Trust property and is inhabited by about 12 people. Holiday accommodation is available. Contact: Lundy Office, The Quay, Bideford, for information on boat trips and accommodation. Tel. 01237 470422.

Walk 16: Barnstaple to Bideford via The Tarka Trail

Grid Reference: SS 557327

Distance: 9 miles (13½km)

Terrain: Very easy

Refreshments: Cafés and pub lunch facilities in both towns and the Tarka Projects own refreshment carriage and information centre at the Bideford end of the walk. At the far side of Bideford Bridge, over the River Torridge, Tanton's Hotel caters specially for non-resident walkers.

Starting Point: Barnstaple Junction Station

There is a car park at Barnstaple Junction railway station, or a regular bus service. This is a relatively new walk and cycleway, once the rail route between the two towns and some villages in between. The walk can also be extended beyond Bideford to Torrington and the villages of Merton and Meeth, all part of the Henry Williamson *Tarka the Otter* experience. At the outset do be aware that this route is also a cycleway and that few cyclists seem to have bells on their bikes these days.

Walk out of the car park **beneath** the bridge arch which takes you under the main road and then left through a metal gateway to strike westwards toward Bideford. There are Tarka information boards on your left and a straight path stretches before you. In fact, this path continues without deviation all the way to Bideford, excepting at Instow where you cross the road. It is well-signed throughout.

At the first "Cyclists Ring Your Bell" sign on your left are exits off the trail to left and right. Our first mysterious area is along the track to the left where you go through another metal gate to find a dripping well on your left. This ancient healing well has water which is good for the eyes. In 1865 it was built up with stonework as part of a landscape feature by the Sir Bourchier Wrey Estate which extended from here to Tawstock Court and beyond. This is the Anchor Woods Dripping Well.

In recent times the water has been analysed, the formula found to be rich in minerals good for the eyes! The ancients certainly knew what they were about. Monks dressed in dark grey habits have been seen here by the well on rainy days, a haunting which exists to this day with sightings into the 1990s. There is also a peculiar brown, furry creature of about 1½ metres (4-5ft) tall which glides up the path from the well and into the woods to disappear amongst the trees. Recent sightings have been at Midsummer, during the night, the Yeti-like creature even showing brown in the dark. I have interviewed a young man who saw it whilst working the woods with a friend and two lurcher dogs, looking for rabbits, in 1995. The dogs would not budge on seeing the apparition, the

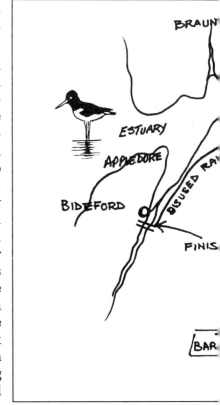

two men running from the scene in some fear rather than investigate the phenomenon. This was their second sighting in two years, both in late June. Other tales of such sightings go back over many years, the apparition always disappearing at the same point in the woods.

Retrace your steps to the Tarka Trail and left towards Bideford with the River Taw on your right. The Taw, and the Torridge at Bideford, are the two sister rivers referred to by Williamson in his Tarka story, and famous as a wader and wildfowl refuge. Just north across the river from here you will see a stone building close to the water's edge. This is the Heanton Court Hotel on the Barnstaple to Braunton road, and also haunted. But that's another walk.

Continue on along the trail, the track gradually heading into a cutting and beneath a road bridge. In spring the banks are an

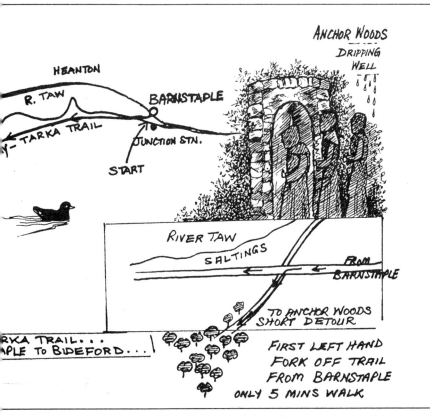

ANCHOR WOODS
DRIPPING WELL
HEANTON
R. TAW
BARNSTAPLE
TARKA TRAIL
JUNCTION STN.
START
RIVER TAW
SALTINGS
FROM BARNSTAPLE
TO ANCHOR WOODS
SHORT DETOUR
RKA TRAIL...
PLE TO BIDEFORD...
FIRST LEFT HAND
FORK OFF TRAIL
FROM BARNSTAPLE
ONLY 5 MINS WALK

absolute mass of primroses, a superb sight. Go on to where an iron bridge crosses a tributary of the Taw. This is Fremington Creek, or Pill, with the village of that name just a shortish walk up the track on either side. If you are considering a meal or drink at the village, cross the bridge and go left along the path under the trees as this brings you out directly opposite the New Inn. If not, continue on to Instow, a seaside village with sand-dunes. The chalets we pass here are let to summer visitors. There are some pretty views here across the estuary to Braunton Burrows and Appledore village on different sides of Bideford and Barnstaple Bay. The whole river is an SSSI for its wildlife importance. (Site of Special Scientific Interest).

At the Bideford end of this part of the Tarka Trail are some railway carriages, now the Information Centre and refreshment area provided by Devon County Council. Alternatively, you can cross Bide-

Instow sands

ford Bridge to Tanton's Hotel to the left as you come off the bridge. Tanton's are pleased to see walkers and you may have a meal and drink here at your leisure as non-residents. Ask there for details of their special walking weekends.

Bideford was the home of a notorious witch, Temperance Lloyd, who, with two companions, was convicted of sorcery at Exeter in 1682. It appears she had a long-standing reputation for malevolence and had been tried and acquitted on similar charges previously. Rather foolishly she boasted she had brought about the deaths of many Bideford people and this secured her conviction, even though prosecuting evidence was the usual stuff of devil-pacts and witches familiars. All three were convicted and hanged.

Also at Bideford it seems the Devil and the Virgin Mary could not agree (surprise! surprise!) over the site of the bridge over the Torridge and each night the Devil destroyed the work done by day. Eventually the builders used woolpacks instead of stone for the pier foundations and got so much work done in a day that the silt and debris build-up was such that Old Nick couldn't destroy it at night. Thus the job was swiftly completed and the Devil thwarted.

Walk 17: Hartland - Stoke - Spekes Mill (North Devon)

Grid Reference:	SS 225248
Distance:	5½ miles (8km)
Terrain:	Coastal path and road. Steep climbs in places.
Refreshments:	Docton Mill (at times) or Hartland Quay Hotel
Starting Point:	Hartland Quay

Hartland has a history of wrecks and smuggling, the former even in recent times. The best-known centre on the Danish captain of a ship wrecked in a storm off Hartland Point, a man named Coppinger. He survived the wreck and lived on a local farm where he married the owner's daughter and settled until his father-in-law died. Inheriting the farm, Coppinger soon became 'Cruel' Coppinger, leader of a group of wreckers and smugglers. His reputation as a cruel and ruthless character was well earned. It is said he eventually decided to retire and, taking his booty, he was last seen hailing a large ship that lay offshore by the Gull Rock. A boat collected him and the ship made sail and left, neither Coppinger nor the ship were heard of again.

Hartland Point was once the Headland of Hercules, legend saying that Hercules landed here in a golden boat, fought with giants and for some years governed the whole region. Hartland Quay Hotel is about 2½ miles west from the village and has fine views, food, drink and a convivial atmosphere.

From here walk up the road to turn left at the signpost and head north, with the sea on your left. At a ruined tower go down into the valley and just before the stream, turn right, heading inland away from the coast. Go up along the waymarked route towards the church, where views take in some wind-blasted trees.

Go onto the road here and left towards the church. It is well worth a look around inside. There is a fine 'Arthurian' stained glass window and links with St Nectan, the much revered saint of this

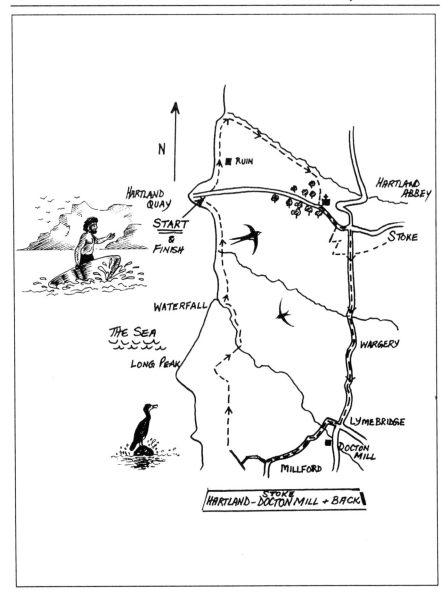

part of Devon and Cornwall. Just along the road you will find St Nectan's Well, always worth a visit for the absolute peace to be found there, a peace of spirit, a holy place indeed.

St Nectan is still seen by some here near the well, whilst others claim to clearly hear a silver bell chiming at the St Nectan's Kieve near Tintagel in Cornwall. Of King Brychan, who gave his name to Brecon in Wales, Nectan was decapitated by robbers but picked up his head, walked to his well and dropped it in. Wherever the ground was sprinkled with his blood, foxgloves sprang up. Now, on St Nectan's Day, 17th June, mass is still celebrated at the well, local children marching in procession, carrying foxgloves.

But we must move on. Past the church and around the corner the road turns left, then right into Stoke village. Just beyond the right turn, on the right, is a gap between houses. Follow the path south and straight on at the crossroads, along a lane with high Devon hedgebanks on each side, then a field beyond. Follow the road downhill to Lymebridge where you turn right at the road junction signed Docton Mill with a lovely little stream alongside. During the summer you can obtain refreshments here.

Go on uphill beyond the mill and take the second public footpath on the right which takes you to another steep downhill slope. There are wonderful views from here before your descent, then go downhill towards a bridge over the stream, with an open area meeting up with the coastal path. The stream here pours over as a wonderful cascade to the sea. Just to your left is Long Peak.

Turn right (north) and climb the steps up out of the valley, over the top and down into the next valley with the clearly waymarked path passing an earthworks to go round the back of a sheer outcrop. Climb again to find Hartland Quay and rooftops guiding you back down the path to the pub. A fine walk!

Walk 18: Croyde – Baggy Point – Putsborough – Woolacombe

Grid Reference: SS 435395
Distance: 5½ miles (8km)
Terrain: Coastal path. Some hills but not difficult – 5 stiles.
Refreshments: Croyde, Putsborough and Woolacombe
Starting Point: National Trust car park

This is a linear walk with parking at each end so it can be done in reverse or you can walk back again to the starting point, or catch a bus from Woolacombe back to Croyde – it is a frequent service.

For the lover of sea views and coastal flora and fauna this is a magnificent walk with well-maintained footpaths. At the NT car park, walk uphill away from Croyde (north-west) and you will find yourself at a gateway onto the coastpath. Go through and follow the path by a hotel or tea gardens on the right. Note the remains of a whale skeleton here on your right, the whale was washed up on the beach in 1915.

Walk on to a NT gate and superb sea views out to the left. Out at sea, the lighthouse flashing is Hartland Point and ahead of you is the island of Lundy, the Puffin Isle. Go on along the cliff path with the sea and rugged rocks below you on the left. Do not stray off the path. Ahead is a shelf of rock jutting out from the cliff, this is a geologically important raised beach and worth a photograph. Below to your left the black rock close inshore is Shag Rock and you may see shags and cormorants perched upon it. The coast here is noted for its seabird colonies during the breeding season.

Walk on to Baggy Point, heeding the NT safety barrier and signs. Landslips do occur and the sheer cliffs are not to be explored. A right turn takes you up a steep but short path to the first of five stiles. You are now above the Wreckers' Path, above Seal Cavern, a landmark of the *Tarka the Otter* story. The ghostly figure of a wrecker is sometimes seen here, and along the cliff edges towards Whiting

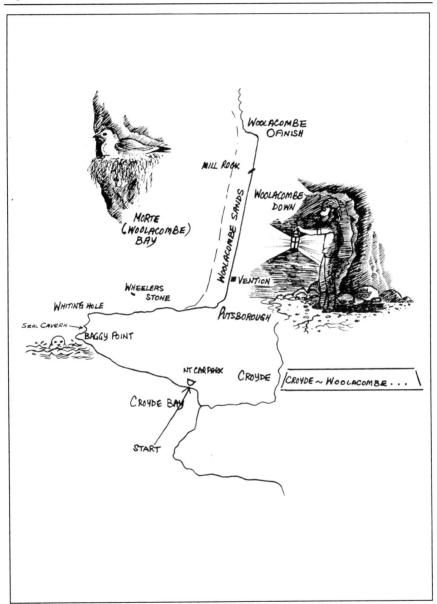

Hole, the figure of a man waving a lantern to attract ships onto the dangerous, rocky coast in order to loot them.

Go over the stile and keeping a wire fence to your left, head in away from the cliff edges towards the stone wall, turning left to follow the wall which is now immediately on your right.

The coast path is well defined here on the sward so walk on east with lovely views of the sea and Morte Point away to the north. You will see Woolacombe in the distance in the north, but it is not as close as it looks. Your path passes the Wheelers Stone and Long Bar as you progress towards Putsborough, always holding to the path closest to the cliff edge as it were. Now follow the steep downward path to the Putsborough car park and go over the stile into it to find toilet facilities beneath the old pine trees and a refreshment chalet close to the beach if you need it. Go out of the car park at the north-east end through a gateway onto a road and cross the road to go down to a fork. Here a grass track goes to a gate on the right off the road. Follow this and go through the gate and on above Vention House, a delightful horseshoe-shaped property down to your left. Go on across the field here towards two gates and a stile leading on to a track. Go over and turn left, following the track north. Do not deviate onto the right-hand routes which will take you inland and off course. Looking back south and south-west here you will see the wonderful views of the route you have just walked.

The sands below to your left as you go on towards Woolacombe are Woolacombe Sands. These are mentioned elsewhere as those haunted by the ghost of William de Tracy who weaves his rope of sand here, himself haunted by the Black Hound carrying the ball of fire in its jaws, ready to burn the rope if it ever nears completion.

You are now walking below Woolacombe Down. Continue on along the now wide and rather stony path which becomes a car park area along the seaward side, and then go left out of the car park onto the metalled road and pavement route into the village. There are a number of inns, cafés and hotels here for food and refreshments, and a coach and bus park to your right.

Walk 19: Zeal Monachorum – Down St Mary

Grid Reference:	SX 722037
Distance:	4½ miles (6.5km)
Terrain:	Easy but hilly
Refreshments:	Zeal Monachorum
Starting Point:	The Waie Inn

We can't omit Zeal Monachorum from a book of mysterious walks for the White Bird of the Oxenhams has to be one of the strangest tales in Devon, even sparking off a TV film in the West Country some years ago. The Oxenhams lived in a remote farmhouse in the parish of Zeal. Twenty-two-year-old John Oxenham fell sick and died after seeing a strange white bird hovering over himself. Two days later the wife of his brother James died after seeing a similar apparition, swiftly followed by her sister, Rebeccah, aged 8 who also saw the bird. Then the baby of James and Thomazine (who had just died) also died. Four lives had been lost in a matter of days, and the bird had presented itself to at least three of the doomed people. Four other members of the family who were taken ill, recovered and none of these reported seeing the bird.

It is also said that Grace, the grandmother of John Oxenham, had seen such a white bird as she lay dying in 1618. In 1743 William Oxenham saw the bird outside his bedroom window and vowed it would not claim him, but he died anyway. At Sidmouth in the early 1800s another member of the family died even as others were at his deathbed, knowing nothing of such a legend, but all saw the white bird fly across the room. Then in 1873, G.N. Oxenham, a family member residing in Kensington, saw the white bird in a tree outside his window. He, too, died shortly afterwards. Sightings of the bird continued in the 20th century, though some members of the family were extremely sceptical. Scepticism aside, it is a most interesting and bizarre tale which may still resurrect itself from time to time.

So on to our walk. Turn left outside the inn and go up the lane that passes the garden until you reach the River Yeo, one of several

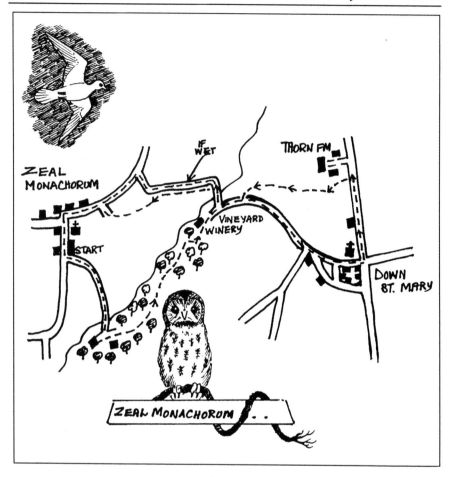

so named in Devon. Pass the bridge, turn left and walk along the riverbank, through the trees, to the far side of a quarry, where the track goes on to a gate. Go through the gate and on along the bottom of the field, keeping close to the river along two fields and holding to the path as it rises through pine trees. Keep on in the same direction, and down to the river again, over a stile towards farm buildings. Go on by an open-sided barn and over another stile near a thatch-roofed house and along a lane to the road. This is the Down St Mary Winery where you may taste and buy the local product.

Go east along the road out of the valley, uphill to Down St Mary.

It ought to be 'Up St Mary' but 'dun' was Saxon for a hill. There are good views from here and that is Dartmoor to the south. Go on to the church, keeping left as you reach the village green, to turn left at the corner of the churchyard. Go along the lane by Marydowne House on the left and come to Thorne Farm on the left. Now follow the well waymarked route leaving the road shortly before the farm and going left around a number of fields and over a few stiles. Once at Middle Yeo Farm, go up the track left to the road, to turn right and go down to the vineyard area again. Follow the road over the bridge, going left up the valley side. Just before the top is a footpath sign pointing the way over a stile, the path running parallel with the left side of the road. At the top corner a stile beside a telegraph pole leads into a field. Keep going with the hedge on your right, and where it ends in the next field go down into the shallow combe. There in the bottom hedge is another stile. Go over and walk up the steep hill to follow a hedge up to a gate, going through to a track on the right which goes through between farm buildings to the road. This is the top of Zeal Monachorum. Turn left and go by the church, back to the starting point.

Walk 20: Salcombe, South Devon

Grid Reference: SX 741392
Distance: 5 miles (7km)
Terrain: Very easy and different – with a ferry trip.
Refreshments: Salcombe
Starting Point: North Salcombe car park by Gould Road

Walk to Gould Road then left to go along Island Street to the end, crossing the road to follow the footpath along the river's edge. Turn right and walk along Fore Street, going straight on at the crossroads. Go left between Salcombe Hotel and the Midland Bank and down the steps to the pier to cross Salcombe harbour by the ferry. Salcombe is aptly named as it is a saltwater 'drowned' river valley. The castle dates from Henry VIII and during the Civil War was for a while named 'Fort Charles', as the last fortress in England to fall to the Roundheads.

In a field above the town the ghost of a lady in grey appeared to a farmer ploughing the land and where she stood, one of his plough oxen sank into the ground. The farmer dug down at the spot to find considerable treasure lying there. The farmer, who was struggling to make ends meet, prospered from then on and it is said that he was able to give each of his children £1500 when they wed. A huge sum in the early 1800s!

Once over the ferry, and don't try walking across, go up the steps to turn right along the lane and go on by Mill Bay, crossing the mouth of the bay to turn right through woodland, with Salcombe harbour and castle opposite. Now follow the lovely cliff walk along Portlemouth Down, which is a series of fields, for about 2¼ miles towards Gara Rock. Pass the circular white building and keep left past Gara Rock Hotel, through the car park and along the lane. About 200 metres past the hotel go left through a gate signed 'Mill Bay' and go along the left of the field to a stile. Go over the stile, over the field and over another stile by a gate to turn right towards the farm along

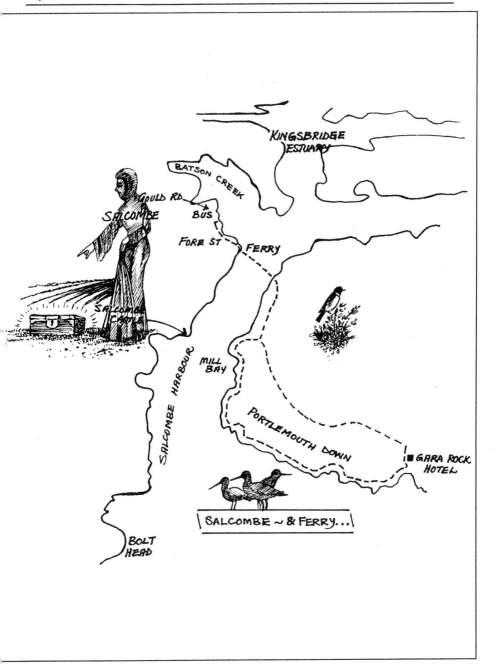

KINGSBRIDGE ESTUARY

BATSON CREEK

GOULD RD

SALCOMBE

BUS

FORE ST

FERRY

SALCOMBE CASTLE

SALCOMBE HARBOUR

MILL BAY

PORTLEMOUTH DOWN

GARA ROCK HOTEL

BOLT HEAD

SALCOMBE ~ & FERRY...

the fenced track. Walk for about 50 metres then turn left along the rough, narrow track, ignoring the gate and track on the left.

After another 150 metres, when at the farm track, turn immediately left, signed to Mill Bay, and when there turn right along the road to the ferry and back to Salcombe.

Walk 21: Axmouth to the Lyme Regis Undercliff

Grid Reference: SY 256911

Distance: 7 miles (10km)

Terrain: Tough. One way. Bus back to Axmouth.

Refreshments: Axmouth and Lyme Regis

Starting point: Harbour Inn, Axmouth harbour.

If you are driving around Devon in order to find our starting points, consider leaving your vehicle at Lyme, catching the bus to Axmouth then doing the walk to your car. Lyme, of course, is in Dorset, but beautifully so.

To the north of Axmouth is an ancient hill fort where a ghostly warrior haunts the site, guarding the Icknield Way and the track that became the Roman Fosse Way. Look for the hill fort on Hawkesdown Hill. A witch at Axmouth, one Charity Perry, was made ill by an Exeter white witch for causing illness to cattle, a sort of tit for tat witchcraft battle. Local youngsters thought Charity left her bedroom via a window each night on a broomstick. It is said she kept a box filled with toads under her bed.

From the Harbour Inn walk to the left, passing St Michael's Church opposite. This is built on an ancient sacred site. King Beorn of the Angles was actually murdered here in 1049 and afterwards taken to Winchester for re-burial.

Fork to the right along Chapel Street, passing Kemp's Lane on the left and Glenwater Close on the right. Go up Stepps Lane to pass a public footpath on your left. Go sharp right along a signed bridleway to the South Devon Coast Path and turn left at the signed junction to Lyme Regis.

Thus far the walk has been easy, but once you enter the magical Undercliff you will find the going tough as the nature reserve signs clearly inform you. The route is easy to follow, however, and well waymarked, but if you normally time yourself on the basis of 3½ miles to an hour's walking, then do add an hour for the 7 miles trip.

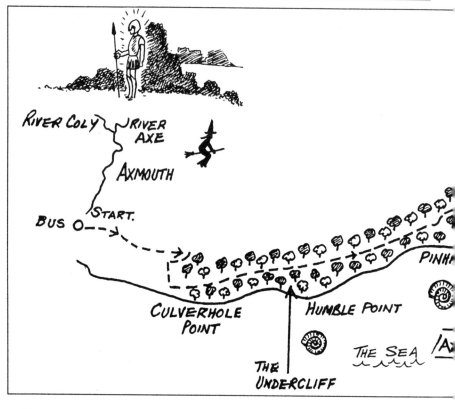

Follow the path to the sea, with excellent birdlife, butterflies and wildflowers to be found along the way.

On reaching the National Nature Reserve information board, go over the stile into the Undercliff. At the signed route left to Lyme Regis, follow the path for about 20 paces and go right up the waymarked route. Ignore any map routes to the contrary and keep away from cliff edges! You will reach a water pumping station and sign. Go on along the coast path to Lyme Regis and then where the track climbs up to Pinhay, you fork right with the waymarked Coast Path route to eventually arrive at another NNR information board.

Go along the lane ahead, ignoring the right hand farm turning, passing a bungalow to come to a signpost. Go right through a kissing gate then on to another kissing gate and into the county of Dorset,

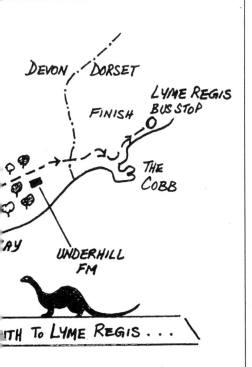

with fine sea views to your right. Now follow the signed coast path, bearing right to cross a stream and following a hedge on your right. Now turn right and go over a stile to go down to The Cobb at Lyme Regis, walking left to pass the harbour and beach on your right. You then reach The Square in Lyme Regis. Here there is a bus service to Axmouth, or to Seaton on Sundays and Bank Holidays.

In the 17th century, one Mayor Jones of Lyme Regis was rather cranky with his persecution of non-conformists following the Restoration, driving local dissenters from the town. They used to visit White Chapel Rocks on Pinhay Cliffs to hold services, with Mayor Jones lurking above the cliff path, in what was known as Jones's Chair, noting names. When Jones died the Devil sent a ship to fetch him and this Devil-ship was hailed by a passing vessel. In answer to the ship's queries the response was, "Sailed from Lyme, skipper's name Satan, cargo Old Jones, Mount Etna destination." The Devil-ship then disappeared in flames.

Lyme Bay is famous for its fossils and beloved of Jane Austen. It was here in 1811 that 12-year-old Mary Anning found the fossilised Ichthyosaurus at Black Ven, along this very shoreline.

Walk 22: Exmouth to Budleigh Salterton, Littleham and back

Grid Reference: SY 001811

Distance: 11 miles (5km)

Terrain: Some ups and downs but easy

Refreshments: Exmouth, and at Budleigh Salterton

Starting Point: From the South Western Inn

Exmouth, situated nicely on the coast not far from Exeter, has a lot of interest for the walker visitor and is useful as a 'rainy day' walking area, but excellent for fine day walking as well – it is Devon's oldest resort. The South Western will appeal to railway enthusiasts, especially thirsty ones, and there are other watering holes nearby, as indeed there are at Budleigh Salterton, en route.

Here at Exmouth there is a peculiar haunting. Belmont House in Bicton Street was once, and may still be, haunted by the crying child of Rev Jonas Dennis and his wife Juliana, a boy who died aged 2 from a long illness following a fall which injured his head. On the night the coffin lid was screwed down the maid and some of the family clearly heard the child calling, and this continued for several days. On one occasion his sister Maria saw the apparition of her brother's hand appear through the unglazed door window of the attic room where he lay. The coffin was buried in the garden, however, with no further investigation, until the cook said she had seen a headless figure enter the kitchen and go into the pantry, to suddenly vanish. The child's body was then exhumed, examined to confirm the cause of death and reburied. The house's reputation as being haunted continued, as might be expected. But on to our walk.

Cross the road and go left, then bear right passing the Memorial Garden on your left. Go left up the Strand, bearing right at the roundabout to reach The Beacon Road forking left. You take the signed Plantation Walk nearby to bear right at a fork which brings you out beside The Deer Leap Inn. Now cross the road and go left

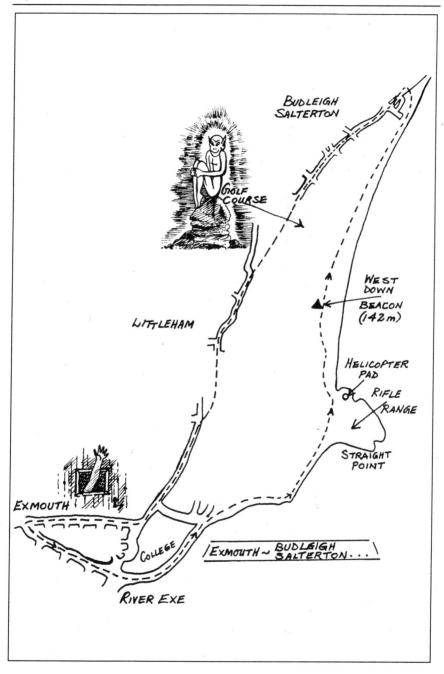

along the seafront with the beach on the right, passing the lifeboat and the Works of Miniature on your left.

Go left when the road forks, turning right at the crossroads to walk along Foxhole Hill by the car park. Now go right along the signed coast path to Sandy Bay and Budleigh Salterton along a well-maintained path above the beach on the right. Continue on past holiday chalets on the left to the Beachcombers' Bar. The coast path now takes you by the Royal Marine ranges on the right and past the helicopter landing pad with fine views of the red sandstone cliffs beyond. Follow the path across West Down Beacon for about 142 metres and go downhill to Budleigh Salterton.

If time permits a visit to the Fairlynch Museum is worthwhile and here, too, is the excellent South Devon Seabird Trust which does such fine work rehabilitating oiled seabirds. We are now in Sir Walter Ralegh country, and Millais painted the famous Boyhood of Ralegh here at Budleigh Salterton. The town's name by the way means 'Budda's forest clearing and salt pans', the latter once being worked at the mouth of the River Otter.

Pixies live in the woods around Budleigh Salterton, one Ruth Tongue recording an incident when a woman from Nettlecombe in Somerset was pixie-led and could not find her way out of the wood even though the way "was plain to see". Eventually someone went to find her and all was well.

On with the walk, pixie-led or not. Turn left along South Parade and into Fore Street, with the octagon house on your right (Millais). Now go by the T.I.C. and the King William IV Inn on your left to continue up West Hill. At the top, pass Links Road and as the Exmouth road bears right, go on to the signed Littleham church path. Pass the golf course and take the path through the kissing gates into the corner of a field, following the right-hand hedge to the signpost. Take the Littleham path over open country to another kissing gate in the hedge. On crossing the golf course to a track which bears left to follow the signed Littleham church path, follow the yellow waymarked route. Then go left into the woodland walk to reach a stile, crossing this to a road called Castle Lane.

Go left down to Littleham, past the church and right up Littleham

Road. Then go left down Elm Lane, passing a school on the right to follow the public footpath ahead to metal kissing gates.

Littleham is on the route of the famous Devil's Footprints of 1854-5, a bitter winter with much snow and tough conditions. A line of weird footprints went from Totnes eastwards, visiting Torquay, Dawlish and other places near the Exe estuary, including Exmouth. Drawings made at the time were a mix of cloven-hoofed and horse-shoe-like sketches, the media making much of the Devil running about the Devon countryside, obviously with mincing steps as the track were said to be between 15 and 20cms (6-8 inches) apart. (See Mysterious Bits and Pieces chapter.)

Now go on beside a hedge on your right, crossing a stile by a gate in the corner. Pass Green Farm on your right to go on through another kissing gate to follow the stream on your left. After yet two more kissing gates, go right away from the stream to a kissing gate between two field gates in the hedge ahead. Now follow the enclosed path to a junction and turn right to bear left with the hedgerow path. Ignore the stile on your right. On reaching the road go left down Douglas Avenue, then right along Rolle Road and straight on at the roundabout to find the town centre and your starting point.

Walk 23: Dartmouth – The Castle – Blackstone Point – Little Dartmouth and back

Grid Reference: SX 878511

Distance: 5½ miles (8km)

Terrain: Hilly. Coastal path and road. Easy.

Refreshments: Dartmouth

Starting Point: Dartmouth, Agincourt House

There is a good bus service from Dartmouth to Totnes and Dartmouth is also close to the famous Dart Valley Railway. Agincourt House (14th-century) is next to The Dartmouth Arms and is haunted by two ghosts which isn't a bad start, whilst on Dartmouth Quay at The Royal Castle Inn, a coach and horses rattles over the cobbles outside (and partly inside!) so watch your feet if you're having a drink when it appears. It is thought the coach may be that of Mary, consort of William III, arriving to take her from her lodgings to meet her husband at Torbay. Dartmouth is a naval town of great historical importance, and with the Britannia Royal Naval College here today, there are constant links with the sea – so a nautical flavour to our walk.

Go to the right with the harbour on your left to Bayard's Cove Fort, going through to its far end and turning right up the steps to the road. Turn left above the Dart estuary on your left, bearing left at the fork and along Warfleet Road. Then go left along Castle Road and left again along the lower road to the castle. The castle lies by the Dart estuary, evidently the first castle in England built with gun batteries in mind, in 1481. The castle is under the aegis of English Heritage.

Now climb steps to the high road and go left, passing the picnic site on the left. Go down the steps along the cliff path through the trees and walk down Sugary Cove and up the path meandering through the woods. Bear left at the junction. Follow the lane for a

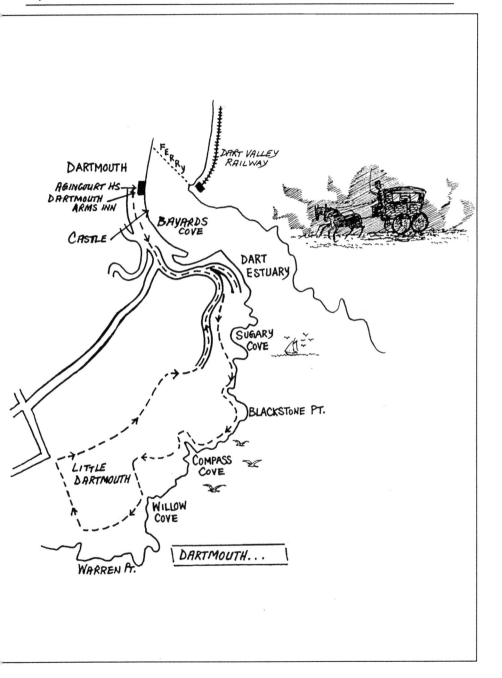

DARTMOUTH

AGINCOURT HS
DARTMOUTH
ARMS INN

CASTLE

FERRY

DART VALLEY
RAILWAY

BAYARDS
COVE

DART
ESTUARY

SUGARY
COVE

BLACKSTONE PT.

LITTLE
DARTMOUTH

COMPASS
COVE

WILLOW
COVE

WARREN PT.

DARTMOUTH...

short distance and go left along the signed coast path to Little Dartmouth.

Go downhill to Blackstone Point and keeping close to the sea, cross the footbridge over an inlet, climbing above Compass Cove. Continue along the coast path through a gateway, passing a right-hand stile, and along the cliff top path leading to another footbridge. Go on round the hillside and through the gap in the wall to turn right and follow the wall.

Turn right, walking inland along a fence line. Go through the kissing gate and along the left side of fields until you reach the NT car park. Now go right along the signed bridleway to Dartmouth. This can be muddy at rainy times, but then so can most walks. After Little Dartmouth, continue over the stile and along the bridleway waymarked in blue. That's novel. Now go along the road from the coastguard cottages and follow it back to Dartmouth and your starting point.

Walk 24: Loddiswell, along the Primrose Line to Avon Mill and back

Grid Reference: SX 720486

Distance: 3½ miles (5km)

Terrain: Disused railway and road. Short and easy.

Refreshments: Loddiswell and Avon Mill

Starting Point: The Loddiswell Inn

The Loddiswell Inn is doubly haunted. Look for an old man who is seen sitting by the fire in the corner of the bar. Don't prod to see if the apparition disappears, it may be a customer! At the foot of the steps leading up from the bar to the restaurant, the ghost of a lady dressed in grey is sometimes to be seen haunting the inn, which was once called The Turk's Head. I wonder if it was named after the Turk's Head Lily sometimes seen growing in Devon? I must say I found this walk delightful in springtime and the Avon Mill coffee shop a fine place for refreshments.

So let's move on to this welcome spot. From the inn go right then turn right along the main Loddiswell road, passing the sports field on the left and Ham Butts Lane on your right. Pass Loddiswell Butts Road junction on your left and continue on by the access lane to Ham Farm on the right. Turn right along a signed public path which is a joy of wildflower and birdlife as you walk between Devon hedgerows down into woodlands, bearing left to cross the stream here.

Cross the river over the old railway bridge and turn right along the old rail route then walk through woodland above the lovely River Avon on your right. Where the path approaches a gate, turn left over the stile, turning immediately right to follow the narrow path to the road. The old rail route is on the right. Go over the stile at the end to the road at the old Loddiswell railway station.

Now go right down the road, ignoring the track bearing right to Rake Farm, and bear right at the crossroads and under the old rail bridge. Go through the gate in the hedge right to follow the path across the field with the river on your right. Turn right across the road bridge over the river and proceed on past Avon Mill Coffee Shop and the Rural Crafts Gallery on the right. (Or stop and browse for a while.) Go on uphill to a junction, bear right up the track, then

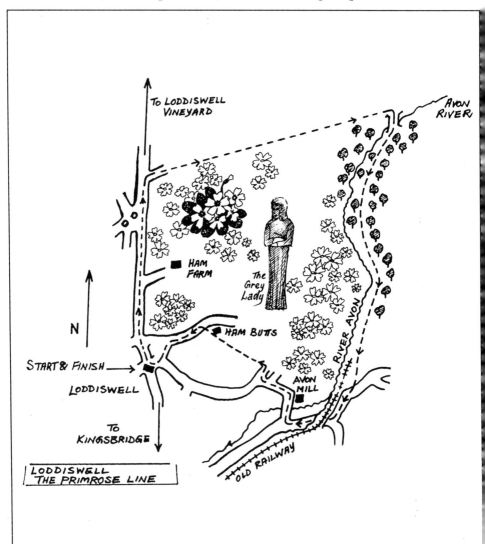

left to continue along the track between hedges to the Ham Butts crossroads.

Turn left, signed for Loddiswell, and follow the lane past St Michael's Church on the left. Fork left and walk on to the village centre and your starting point.

With Kingsbridge just to the south of Loddiswell, and the old Primrose Line here so delightfully alive with snowdrops, celandines, daffodils, primroses and bluebells from early spring onwards, you are well placed to enjoy the very best of gentle Devon and some happy walking.

Walk 25: Tiverton and the Tiverton Canal

Grid Reference: SX 955125
Distance: 7 miles (10km)
Terrain: Easy circular walk for all
Refreshments: Tiverton
Starting Point: Bus station (ample car parking in the area)

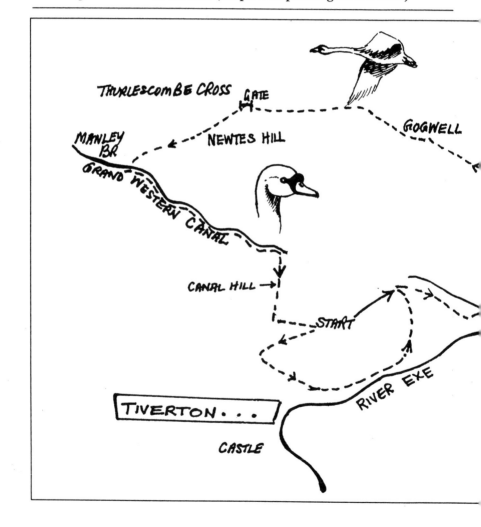

Once a prosperous wool town as a centre of the cloth trade, Tiverton is an attractive, well-kept town today. Whilst one would not wish to speak good of property fires, it is a fact that a series of disastrous fires saw the town centre rebuilt in the Georgian style that helps mark its attractiveness today. 600 houses were burnt in a fire in 1598, 300 in 1731.

Old Baker lived here, a white witch or wizard famed for all things magical from curing warts to being consulted by magistrates in witchcraft cases. In the early 1800s witch trials were common throughout Devon if farm stock became ill and crops failed. Stories of cattle leaping up 2 metres before falling dead upon the ground, and of children falling into fires are part of country tales steeped in superstition, magic, and facts.

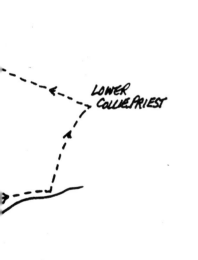

At nearby Chettiscombe is a haunted chapel site where lay a vast treasure guarded by several ghosts. It was said anyone brave enough to stay overnight would be shown the location by one of these apparitions. Two farmers decided to do so and when a 'ghost in the form of a white owl' landed in the field they dug down and found a huge treasure trove! This happened so frequently throughout Britain it is incredible that there are still sceptics about.

Blundell's School is here at Tiverton with many famous pupils becoming legends in the West Country. Parson Jack Russell of Jack Russell terrier fame, who became curate of Swimbridge in North Devon, was taught here, as was Jan Ridd of *Lorna Doone* according to the R.D. Blackmore tale of Exmoor and beyond.

Tiverton's Oak Apple Revel featured effigies of King Charles and Oliver Cromwell being carried through the town and meeting in the town centre in a mock battle. Prisoners taken were ransomed and the money spent in the pubs. The town was decorated with greenery and people wore oak apples and oak twigs in their hats and button-holes. There are perhaps links here with the Green Man.

So, an interesting place to walk as we go up to Fore Street from the bus station car park area and go left, then quickly left again down St Andrew Street. Cross the river to turn right along Colliepriest Road. Just before the buildings at Lower Colliepriest, turn left up a lane which becomes a track and follow this past the house on the right and through the gates, keeping to the left of the last field to a gate on to the road. Cross the road and go along the lane to where it goes down to Gogwell Buildings, turning left here to go along a lane to a road known as Newte's Hill.

Cross the road and go through the gate, crossing the field to its bottom left corner. Go over the stile fence, bearing right to continue down over fields, keeping the hedge on your right. The path now goes between Devon hedges with gates. Go right along the lane and at Thurlescombe Cross go left. Just beyond Manley Bridge, turn right to the canal towpath. Follow the towpath on the right side of the canal and turning right, go down Canal Hill to continue on along Station Road, passing a school on the left. Go down Gold Street. Turn right along Bampton Street then left along Newport Street to the church. Go down St Peter Street then turn left along Fore Street and back to the car park starting point.

Note: Tiverton Canal is owned by Devon County Council and beautifully restored. The 11-mile waterway runs from Tiverton to Loudwell and was completed in 1812. The original plan for a 46-mile canal route was never completed. There is good wildlife watching here along the alder and willow-lined route, with its resident mute swans, moorhens and ducks. A good place to spend time.

Rainy Day Walking

Here are three walks where come rain or shine you'll find some shelter. If it is pouring with rain, or perhaps heavy mists obscure the wilder landscapes, walking in the countryside is less than inviting. No problem. You are in Devon seeking the mysterious so why not a walk around Exeter, an easy city to reach from any part of the county and one with every facility you could wish for on a day of inclement weather – including rain and mist, the ideal conditions for a good haunt!

A wise walker prepares for this eventuality in advance but Tourist Information Centres have a variety of maps including street maps. Exeter's is at the Civic Centre, Paris Road, Exeter (01392 265297). A list of others in Devon are at the back of this book with other useful information.

Walk 26: Exeter

Grid Reference: SX 921925. City street map required
Distance: 5 miles (7km)
Terrain: Road (pavement) walking
Refreshments: Various places about the city
Starting Point: Exeter Catheral

Exeter is an original Dracula location. We have our modern-day stories of the Highgate Vampire and such, but it was here in Devon that Dracula himself selected a solicitor in Cathedral Close to be his agent in England. Transylvania linked with Exeter then, what a tourist attraction! It was Jonathan Harker who was sent to Transylvania to represent the firm of solicitors he worked for, and to Exeter he returned to hide his beloved fiancée from the count. The neckbiter did not discover her in hiding, maybe he still searches.

Visit Exeter's wonderful cathedral, a place of peace in this bustling, ever interesting city which itself was once known as Monk Town. This is perhaps to be expected with the various monastic establishments over the years and both historic and recent reports of ghostly monks haunting properties of all ages. Visit the Cathedral Library for a most extraordinary collection of wax models found in a cavity on top of the stone screen surrounding the choir in the cathedral itself during repairs carried out in 1943.

In 1941 an air raid destroyed much of the old city but the cathedral survived, though it was badly damaged. The wax models included representations of animal and human limbs, part of the head of a horse and the complete figure of a woman. These could be votive offerings once placed on the tomb of Bishop Edmund Lacy who died in 1455. He is said to have shown much saintliness when alive and after his death sick people used to kneel by his tomb praying for recovery, either for themselves or their sick animals. As a symbol of their faith they would leave waxen images of the affected limb or animal. During the Reformation in 1538 the cathedral was cleared of all such relics, but it is likely those found in 1943 had been deliberately hidden by some faithful member of the congregation.

Cathedral Close is haunted by a monk, his dark, cowled figure occasionally seen about at night passing across the Close. Sightings are reported in local newspapers from time to time. Of course, monks seen in or near modern housing areas tend to be haunting the original monastic sites now redeveloped, a useful point for historians and archaeologists to bear in mind. Follow that monk! During 1965 at Wellington Road, monks were observed at at least two houses, whilst yet another haunts the Cowick Barton Inn, at Cowick Lane, Exeter, obviously a connoisseur of good ale. Cowick Barton Inn is built on monastic ground and the monk, affectionately called Fred by the locals, is often seen by day wandering in nearby fields.

But back at the cathedral it is well worth a look inside at the Green Man boss in the nave, a corbel carving of considerable detail representing the Summer Lord or May King, a nature god if you like. There are two Green Man heads tucked away in facing corners of the pulpit, close to the organ. These symbols of glorious nature and fertility are linked with Christ and Christianity, but ancient indeed and absorbed, like so many things pre-Christian, into the Church – along with ancient, sacred wells, springs and other good and natural beliefs and artefacts the Church could not afford to ignore.

Outside, the Globe Hotel in the close is also said to be haunted. One can hear the sound of silks and satins as a lady of the past moves by, going about her ancient business in the old building. She is heard but not seen.

Go to New North Road at St David's, near the railway station. Here at Taddyforde House you can find the old, red sandstone arch of the original entrance to the property. Within the arch itself the former owner, a Mr Kingdon, is said to be buried, and he still appears to people who walk there on occasions. Indeed, even without prior knowledge of the situation, there are those who cannot pass through the arch without shivering uncontrollably. Dowsing on site for evidence of human remains brings a violent reaction from both rod and pendulum and there is a powerful ley running through the archway itself.

Note: Both trains and buses run frequently between Exeter Central and Exeter St David's.

Walk 27: Ilfracombe (Hillsborough) to Mortehoe

Grid Reference: SS 534476

Distance: About 8 miles (12km)

Terrain: Hilly coastal path with superb coastal views and wildlife.

Refreshments: Opportunities at both ends of the walk

Starting Point: Hillsborough car park

This walk is included in the Rainy Day Walking Section because if you do encounter bad weather, Ilfracombe has Chambercombe Manor which is open from April to October. This is an excellent venue for ghostly hauntings in that you can actually walk around the manor interior on guided tours to see the Ghost Room and other items of historic interest. There is also a restaurant in the grounds, and a garden walk. (SS 533468). Chambercombe Manor is well-

Ilfracombe harbour – on a clear day!

signed and is at the end of Chambercombe Road, Ilfracombe, just south of Hillsborough off the A399, and has its own parking facilities.

Let's look at Chambercombe Manor first. Dating from the 11th century and retaining much of its original architecture, it was known to have been in the possession of Sir Henry Champernon, lord of the manor of Ilfracombe in 1162, with mention of a Robert soon after the Norman Conquest. The manor became a farmhouse for many years and in 1865 the then tenant discovered there was a window for which he could not find a corresponding room. Investigations found a hidden room between that once used by Lady Jane Grey and the one adjoining. Within was the skeleton of a woman lying on a bed in the sealed-off chamber, allegedly a titled lady visiting relatives at Chambercombe, and shipwrecked in a storm on the rocks at nearby Hele. It seems she was still alive when brought to the house and put in the room where she later died. The room was then sealed off from the outside world. Today you can see into the room via a glass panel but there is no actual entrance.

The Manor remains haunted and I have spoken to visitors in recent years who heard strange sounds and saw a figure on a staircase during their stay. To this day, in Lady Jane Grey's room (The Coat of Arms Bedroom) a depression often forms in the pillow of the four-poster bed as if someone is lying there. Another visitor to one of the holiday flats told me of seeing "a host of weird gremlin-like creatures dancing in the courtyard one moonlit night". Small, rather fearsome creatures she described them as. There is also a possible history of links with smugglers. It is said that an entrance was found in the early 1900s when excavations near the building revealed a hole large enough for one person to use leading to the underground footway. It is an interesting theory with the north Devon coast having many caves and tiny coves for the beaching of boats carrying contraband from larger vessels offshore. Hele Bay would seem the likeliest link, or the bay between Capstone and Beacon Points. A small entrance fee is payable.

On then to Hillsborough, a good vantage point and the beginning of our walk westwards to Mortehoe. Hele Bay is east from here with

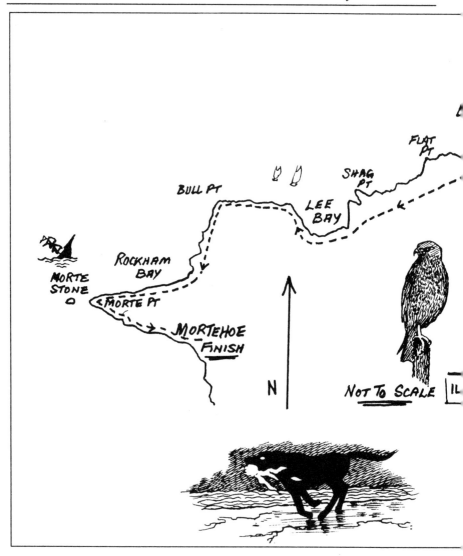

Rillage Point beyond. Hillsborough is 450ft, and one of the few places in the country from which to observe both sunrise and sunset over a seascape. Follow the coast path west to Capstone Point via Ilfracombe harbour. There is a small chapel dedicated to St Nicholas, as patron saint of sailors, on Lantern Hill – an easy climb with

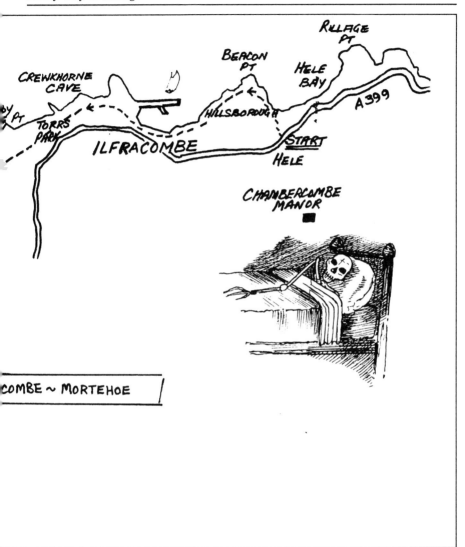

fine views but almost always windy. Then on to Torrs Walks, passing the cliff cave over Crewkherne Cove where William de Tracy once hid from the wrath of Henry II, following his part in the murder of St Thomas of Canterbury in 1170, the infamous murder in the cathedral. A native of this area, de Tracy's ghost now haunts Woolacombe Sands, endlessly attempting to spin a rope from sand. If he seems likely to succeed a black dog appears with a ball of fire in its mouth and burns the cord. In rough weather Sir William rides howling up and down the sands, holding to the local saying that the Tracys 'had every the wind and rain in their faces'.

The next point we come to is Brandy Cove Point, a connection there with smuggling if ever there was one, and then walk on along the coast path, passing Flat Point and Shag Point, the latter named for the green cormorants living and nesting all along the coast here. We are now at Lee Bay with the hotel of that name just along the road if you require refreshment. The rock projecting from the sea here is Pensport Rock. Walk on to Bull Point with its lighthouse, then south-west with lovely views of Rockham Bay. Continue on to Morte Point (death point) with the Morte Stone showing black and ominous from the waves, almost a dreaded warning in itself for several ships have foundered upon it.

It is but a short walk now to Mortehoe village which has an inn and other useful facilities, and buses back to Ilfracombe. William de Tracy lived here at Mortehoe. The great stretch of sands you see stretching south are Woolacombe Sands and bay, with Putsborough Sands in the distance.

Historians may want it said that Tracy and the other three knights who murdered Thomas a Becket were never actually punished for the crime, the King taking the blame upon himself and doing penance publicly at Canterbury Cathedral. In 1173 Tracy was appointed Steward of Brittany, the same year that St Thomas was canonised by the Pope.

Walk 28: Totnes to Windmill Down, Copland Meadow and back

Grid Reference: SX 804604
Distance: 4 miles (6km)
Terrain: Easy
Refreshments: Totnes
Starting Point: The Brutus Stone, Fore Street

Totnes is a pleasant south Devon town with a delightful river and ample facilities for all. A town of character and characters one might fairly say. Indeed, if you are seeking refreshments and ghosts, there is a ghost haunting at The Castle Inn, which used to be the West Gate Tavern in the middle ages. The ghost 'lives' mainly in the cellar so obviously knows real ale.

But here, too, came Brutus, leader of the survivors of the Trojan garrison at Troy, sailing up the River Dart and stepping off on a rock to proclaim,

*"Here I am and here I rest
And this town shall be called Totnes."*

The Brutus Stone, our starting point, is at Fore Street and clearly signed near the old East Gate.

This part of the country was a home of giants and Brutus captured two of these, Gog and Magog, taking them to London where they stood guard outside his palace. The effigies of the two giants are in the Guildhall. The museum in Fore Street houses a display on a more modern legendary character, Charles Babbage, the Totnes 'father' of the computer.

From the Brutus Stone go up through the East Gate arch, out into the High Street, passing St Mary's Church on the right and the Castle Inn on the corner with Castle Street. Now follow the road bearing left then straight on to pass the Bull Inn on your left. Continue to the A381 and cross the road. Go up the lane signed 'Unsuitable for Motors' and then to the road, where you turn right and continue for

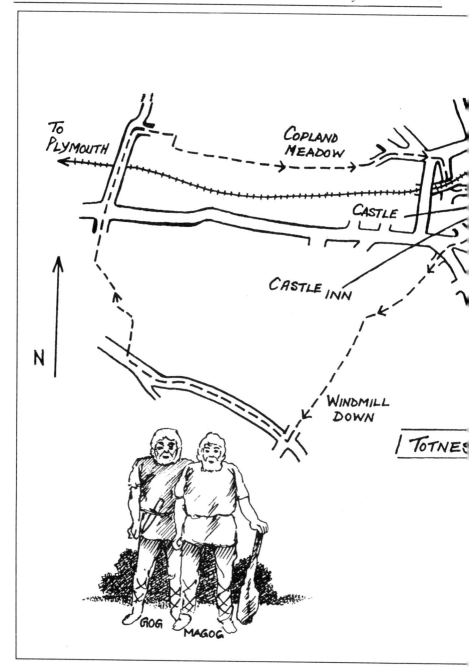

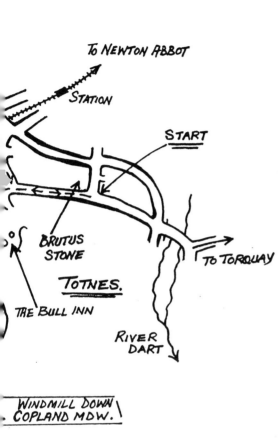

about half a mile. Go right down a track and right again at the fork to reach a crossroads. Continue straight on along the road signed 'Dartington' to eventually cross over a rail bridge. Go right along a green lane to the estate road, Copland Meadow, then go right to the road junction at Barracks Hill, and right again to a T-junction. Cross the road and bear left then quickly right at Malt Mill. Now go under a rail bridge, cross the road and bear left. Now take the right turning with Castle Street and follow the narrow path to Totnes Castle on the right. Continue along Castle Street to turn left into the High Street, through the East Gate and back down Fore Street to the Brutus Stone. Short, sweet and easy.

Totnes is chosen as one of your rainy day walks as it has considerable historic interest including a mint, a cloth industry and a port and was once second only to Exeter in terms of merchant affluence. St Mary's Church is one of Devon's finest with a superb stone screen dated to 1460.

Totnes is now part of a rich farming community and has excellent antique shops and a good number of craftspeople including potters, silversmiths and the like, plus charming river walks and boating. Close to the Butterwalk are the ruins of a 12th-century castle from which to obtain good views over the surrounding area.

Mysterious Bits and Pieces

This short chapter will hopefully enable readers to more fully appreciate and understand some of the phenomena referred to in previous pages. Ghosts or entities which present themselves visually or otherwise can be said to exist – see the discussion later in this chapter. Certainly the British big cats do, and even if there are those that materialise and vanish from sight inexplicably, there are also the very real flesh and blood creatures, not all feline, which inhabit parts of Devon and elsewhere in the British Isles.

Do not be at all surprised at some giant mouse leaping out of a hedgerow or woodland in some secluded, lonely spot. There are wallabies in the county. Do not be surprised if you meet with a ferocious, dark brown, furry, badger-like beast with a furry tail, one that really will take full-grown sheep. There is reliable evidence of wolverines in the West Country and in Wales. Do not be surprised if a puma or a leopard crosses your path, or calls to you from some branch up in a tree whilst you are on a lone woodland walk. There are a few about. I've seen deer carcasses 16ft up in trees! So equally do not be surprised if a large, hairy hand taps you on the shoulder as you walk some misty, eerie track on Dartmoor. It may just be me wishing you a pleasant day.

Berry Pomeroy Castle – A Most Haunted Place Indeed

Just north of Totnes on the road towards Newton Abbot lie the ruins of Berry Pomeroy Castle. Reports of hauntings here can be traced back many years. One eye witness, Sir Walter Farqhal, an eminent physician, was waiting to see a patient at the castle when a beautiful young woman entered the room in an obvious state of distress. She mounted the stairs, turned and looked directly at Sir Walter, then disappeared. Evidently the ghostly woman was the beautiful but wicked daughter of a former owner of the castle, doomed to haunt forever the scene of her evil deeds.

Another haunting is by an illegitimate child who was murdered soon after its birth by the mother, who is believed to be another Pomeroy daughter. The baby's cries are heard and sometimes the baby is seen. The woman herself is said also to haunt the site wearing a long, blue cloak with a hood.

Eleanor de Pomeroy, yet another former owner, also haunts the ramparts in flowing white robes, rising from the dungeon where she starved her sister to death. As recently as 1968 two separate groups of visitors took photographs showing the ghostly figure of a man in a tricorn hat, and the profile of a beautiful woman near the entrance to St Margaret's Tower at the castle. So do visit Berry Pomeroy village, and the castle built by the de la Pomerae family at the time of the Norman Conquest. Haunted it is, and an imposing ruin standing on a shelf above a ravine, amid oaks and beeches.

Even today no one knows the truth of the demise of the building or of the mansion built within its ruined walls by Edward Seymour, the Lord Protector of Somerset. In 1688 William of Orange, on his way to Brixham to become king, came here, yet by 1701 the place lay buried in its own ruins as recorded by the local vicar, John Prince. Fire and lightning were the causes it is said, but there are no true records.

Lydford Castle Hauntings

This information was provided by David Farrant, President of the British Psychic and Occult Society (BPOS) of London, following an investigation of Lydford Castle by members of BPOS during 1985/86.

BPOS was looking into reports of a ghostly sighting near St Michael's Church, Brent Tor, and found there were reports of a ghostly figure at Lydford Castle as well as a black-draped, phantom woman supposedly enticing unwary people to their death in nearby Lydford Gorge. The BPOS members found no trace of the latter other than that of an old, established legend.

However, at the old castle they found an almost over-bearing atmosphere of intense cold and gloom, sensed even before entering the ruined enclosure. Once inside they felt as if they were in a pocket of time, long since forgotten, and felt an intense hostile atmosphere pervading, almost as if warning one to leave. The group reined, returning at night in the hope of gaining some photographic evidence of the 'psychic entity' haunting the ruins. They chose a night of the full moon, a time when psychic forces are most potent and took a year-old Alsatian along with them. The dog immediately 'froze' at the top of the wrought iron staircase leading down to the dungeon, barking repeatedly at something unseen below. The dog had to be carried down and once there, whined continually, cringing in a corner and ignoring all attempts to be pacified.

Just before 3am, a dark shape resembling a large bear was seen to materialise in an adjoining room, appearing to glide several feet before promptly disappearing just below a stone archway. It left behind an intense atmosphere of evil and icy coldness. Attempts were made to photograph the entity, but the film was blank on its return.

The BPOS say that while these occurrences do not provide irrefutable proof of the existence of paranormal activity, they feel it reasonable to state that the investigation succeeded in establishing that local tales of an evil presence in Lydford Castle are not without foundation. The address of BPOS is: 142 Muswell Hill Road, London, N.10.

Of Ghosts and Hauntings

What are ghosts and other strange entities that appear and disappear, haunting indoor and outdoor situations, seen by thousands? Whether some are conjured up psychologically or not, there are those which cannot be explained away as figments of the imagination. For example, if a phantom coach and horses is observed at a particular spot by many people and these observations span many years, maybe a century or two, then that cannot be an imagining. It has to be part of our reality even though we may not entirely understand it.

My own view over many years of studying folklore and legend is that it is due to a set of conditions, even though I cannot explain them scientifically. We all know that many strange phenomena of the ghostly kind occur in dank, misty conditions, eerie conditions if you like, rather than in bright sunshine. This is no accident, I believe it is part of the set of conditions, including some form of natural earth magnetism, the said moist conditions, and an image of the past captured in time. The whole comes together to form a visible picture, quite probably on a ley or earth energy route. In cases of close encounters it is possible that our own body system is electrically receptive, and the reason why a ghost may suddenly disappear could be that the very shock of seeing it has altered our state to one of non-receptiveness. So the ghost becomes invisible, the conditions having altered. Think about it. If, using the example above, a phantom coach always appears at the same place along a particular lane, then why? Why not two miles down the road or halfway to London along its journey? No, the fact that very specific spots are haunted in cases like this has to be down to an exact set of conditions occurring on occasions at that point. And do they occur more frequently, when no one is there to see? We'll never know.

The Devil's Footprints - An Explanation

During 1996, I was invited on to a BBC Radio Devon discussion on the Devil's Footprints – my interests in natural history include the new science of Cryptozoology, the study of 'hidden' animals not as yet formally named by science. The discussion revolved around some serious and some tongue-in-cheek comments on the paranormal and the devil visiting the county. The contributors included well-known investigators such as 'Doc' Shiels of sea-monster photography fame and Jonathan Downes of the Fortsan Centre for Cryptozoology at Exeter.

Evidence of the appearance of the prints in the snow covers a period from the 8th to the 14th of February. 1854-5. By then, just as happens today, some hoaxing may have crept in, but looked at from a naturalist's point of view, I feel the conditions and the prints were those of the bodies of small mammals leaping along seeking food and shelter. Thus the prints were made by a number of these and not one cloven-hooved creature. This would also explain the prints crossing drifting snow and going over the roofs of some sheds and houses as well as the river, which would have been ice-bound at the time.

Over recent years I have seen this phenomenon several times during snow conditions with certain mammal tracks looking remarkably like those referred to. Bear in mind that I refer to the body print as voles or mice leap and bound across the snow, not the footprints of these tiny mammals. This theory has been put forward over several years and is one explanation which tends to cover the facts we have regarding the incident. I should add that on this occasion the other investigators were in agreement. Do listen to BBC Radio Devon whilst exploring our wonderful county.

The Beast of Exmoor

In 1983 the media went wild over reported sheep kills, 'a massacre' said to be caused by a big cat or cats. '80 sheep in 90 days,' said one report, and the Royal Marines were called in to hunt and kill the predators. In fact, there are such cats on the loose in Britain with Exmoor being but one area where they are to be found to this day, even though some have been shot dead.

Pumas and black leopards, or panthers, are two of these cats, and these are certainly escapees and/or releases into the wild from captive situations. I was involved in the Exmoor situation at the outset, but had been aware of pumas on the loose in the West Country since 1967 when a report in the *Western Morning News* stated such a cat was on the loose. Following the 1983 reports on Exmoor, I was more interested in the 'jet black' big cats which I maintain are black leopards, the melanistic form of the spotted leopard, though some say they are black pumas.

Over the years I have seen them, and evidence of them, many times the sightings including adults with cubs, and with subadults. I have become pro-cat over these years, witnessing them taking rabbits when sheep were present nearby on several occasions. I still maintain they are not the sheep killers they are made out to be, though I do agree it was enormously irresponsible of previous owners to allow such a situation to arise. Sadly, the cats get the blame, the owners get away with it.

It wasn't so long ago that puma cubs could be obtained more cheaply than a pedigree dog. I've heard £30 quoted. I've also spoken to previous owners who have 'lost' them or released them. One said when I questioned him about two pumas he owned which he had been told to have put down or given to a zoo, "What would you do with pets you were emotionally involved with?" I know his did not go to a zoo, nor were they put down. I also met a person who said he had released two black African Golden Cats in the Norfolk Broads area because they had started tearing up the furniture fabrics in the house.

It does seem that more and more sightings occurred not so long after the implementation of the Dangerous Wild Animals Act, 1976 which brought in tougher legislation as to how such animals should safely be kept in captivity. It was certainly a tough Act to follow for some pet owners.

If you do meet with one of the cats on your travels then leave well alone. Make no attempt to corner or aggravate it in any way whatsoever. In my experience the animals shun human contact and move off. Letting them do just that is sensible. Whom you inform is your decision. You may wish to let the police know where your sighting occurred. The central switchboard number for Devon is 0990 777444.

I am still investigating the situation and the natural history of the cats in the wild and I am against having them eradicated. If you wish to call me with details please do so on 01271 73520. Thank you.

Other exotic cat species caught or killed in the wilds in Britain in recent times include the Asian leopard cat, the swamp cat or jungle cat, the lynx and the above two named species. The full story is a long one, perhaps I'll write it one of these days. But I hope you see one on your travels. Good luck. And if you're wearing a sheepskin jacket, double good luck.

Another Beast of Exmoor

Werewolves? Who believes in werewolves? Here, for your quiet pondering, is a true story given to me when I was investigating the Exmoor Beast tales which erupted in the early 1980s. The story was subsequently given to the BBC Spotlight News team by the same gentleman, who agreed to relate the story he gave me to the public at large.

The fellow, we'll call him John P, was out rabbiting with his dog, and carrying a loaded shotgun for the purpose of shooting a few rabbits for his supper. He was halfway up a hillside when he heard strange deep-throated growlings and snarlings coming from a dense bramble brake. The sun was just setting and a last chance for supper seemed too good to miss. He set his dog into the brambles "to scare out whatever was in there" and to his horror the noises became blood-curdling mixed with the frenzied barking and snarling of the Jack Russell terrier.

John P said the dog was obviously "in trouble" but he couldn't see it so daren't shoot into the brambles for fear of hitting the dog. Then a shape reared up from the bushes and down again to suddenly look half human, half 'apelike' as it threw the terrier several yards into the open, whilst at the same time emitting bestial snarls. "It stood up and came my way in the gathering darkness of sunset so I shot it," John P said.

With that the hairy creature reared up on its hind legs and remaining upright ran off screaming and roaring, and vanished into the shadows of small trees along a path that goes meandering down to the sea and some small beach areas. John P told me he was sure he'd hit it. He said he rarely misses rabbits and this 'thing' was 5 to 6ft tall when it was upright. He said the face was hair-covered and the hair was down over its shoulders, "just like a werewolf" he claimed.

His dog was scratched about. The main problem was its fear, the hapless animal shivered well into the night before it fell asleep exhausted. He would not go into the area of that hillside ever again, it remembered the incident, said John P. He was a most sincere and serious person and obviously aware how such a story would seem, but equally he was convinced that the cats I was seeking were as nothing compared to this creature, whatever it was. He was also convinced he had shot it and the only reason the creature had run off was that it had been hit. John P agreed to talk to the BBC news people and did so at my home, giving them the same story. It went out later as part of the continuing saga of the so-called Beast of Exmoor.

Since then, in quite recent times, wolverines, the North American gluttons, have entered the picture with sightings in Wales and the West Country of this dark brown, badger-like animal with a longer tail than a badger and reputedly, a ferocious and fearsome reputation as a killer of sheep and other creatures.

I do not think the two creatures referred to are one and the same animal. I do not know what John P saw on that night whilst out rabbiting in North Devon. I do know that the wolverines exist, having seen two of them myself. They were also reported as being in the wild in Wales and farmers were warned to be on the lookout for them. No one seems to know where they have come from, nor where they are at present.

Perhaps you will see them on your travels or even the creature seen by John P. My advice is don't pet them if you do. But tell the Police Wildlife Liaison Officer of the area you are in. Tel. 0990 777444.

Wildlife Notes

The West Country is a stronghold for many wildlife species, despite the general declines across the country due to adverse human pressures. Like Somerset and Cornwall, Devon is an excellent wild-life watching county so if you have binoculars do carry them. From coastal habitats to hinterland, throughout the year, the walker is treated to constant sightings of flora and fauna species.

Gulls, including the lovely kittiwakes; fulmars, shags, oyster-catchers and peregrines are but a few of the coastal nesting species. Here, too, are razorbills and guillemots, rock pipits and ravens, and over on the island of Lundy, puffins and seals. The cliffs are covered in golden gorse, pink thrift and white campion, colourful lichens and in many parts the hanging oakwoods, the trees clinging to the cliffsides and teeming with wildlife.

The estuaries, quieter in summer, are havens for waders and wildfowl from late August to March. Some are Sites of Special Scientific Interest (SSSI) for this very reason. There are always a few waders about even in summer, non-breeding birds and species of wildfowl such as shelduck and mallard which breed close to estuary sites.

Devon's rivers have otters, salmon and trout, kingfishers and wagtails. The faster flowing streams have dippers and all waterways have grey herons fishing along them. An abundance of wildflowers may be found in such places, as well as along country lanes with high Devon hedge banks and many butterfly species.

The moors are known for red deer, the occasional glimpses of ring ouzels and merlins, and always the whinchats, wheatears and redstarts to delight us on our walks. Cotton grass may be a speciality in some areas, whilst gorse and rowan are always to be found. Devon's woodlands, particularly the broad-leaved or deciduous woods, also hold hundreds of wildlife species. You may be walking with willow and wood warblers, chiff chaffs and blackcaps all around you, migrants here for the summer singing along with the resident species – the robins and blackbirds, nuthatches, treecreepers, woodpeckers, wrens and all.

In spring, Devon is about primroses and violets, celandines, bluebells, wood anemones and the like; and in summer the lush vegetation, many fern species and flowers such as foxgloves, enchanters nightshade, willowherb and buttercups.

A walker's wildlife paradise, Devon, but we must not forget the declines, we must not be a part of them by adding to the pressures. Most of us will walk during the breeding season of many species so adhering to footpaths, not straying from them, is the way of the responsible walker and brings us safer guarantees of seeing wildlife in the years to come.

If you are in Devon for a while you may find joining in with a guided walk could add to your day and knowledge. There are many organised by the RSPB and County Wildlife Trusts. Some may fit in with the walks you are planning.

Contact addresses:

RSPB, S.W. Regional Office, 10 Richmond Road, Exeter. Tel: 01392 432691

Devon Wildlife Trust, 35 St David's Hill, Exeter. Tel: 01392 427313

Devon Bird Watching & Preservation Society, P. Ellicott Esq., 10 Chapel Road, Exeter. (County Records only)

National Trust HQ for Devon, Killerton, Exeter. Tel: 01392 881418

Tarka Project, Bideford Old Station (Tarka Trail Information), East-the-Water, Bideford, Devon. Tel: 01237 424625

SOUTH DEVON
WALKS with CHILDREN

Su Stewart

SOUTH DEVON WALKS WITH CHILDREN

Su Stewart

This collection of 25 easy yet stimulating walks covers the area between Exeter in the east and Mount Edgecumbe (just over the Cornish border) in the west. The varied routes explore town and country, moorland, woodland and coast. The author keeps all members of the family entertained by including stories, legends and points of natural and historical interest. Plus vital information - such as location of toilets, shops, telephone numbers and refreshments - to make sure the walk is carefree for parents as well as children! £6.95

TEA SHOP WALKS IN SOUTH DEVON AND DARTMOOR

Norman & June Buckley

Nothing could be more enjoyable than a walk with a welcoming tea shop. And where else can this be better realised than in South Devon, land of fine coastal scenery, glorious Dartmoor and, above all, the world-famed cream tea?

Thirty circular walks have been carefully selected, from Branscombe and Sidmouth almost to Plymouth. Several lengths of the South West Coast Path are included and the lovely fringes of Dartmoor are not neglected. Walks are between two and seven miles, and in the main are gentle rambles using lanes and established footpaths. With clear descriptions, sketch maps, vital information and the authors' own stunning photographs, this book is a must for locals and visitors to Devon. £6.95

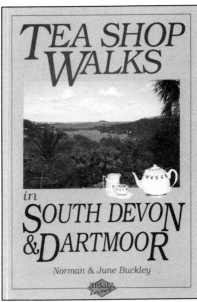

TEA SHOP WALKS
in SOUTH DEVON & DARTMOOR

Norman & June Buckley

TEA SHOP WALKS IN NORTH DEVON
Norman & June Buckley

This is the companion volume to the Buckleys' South Devon Tea Shop Walks. All of the popular areas are covered - from the seaside towns of Ilfracombe and Westward Ho to the delightful inland towns and villages for which North Devon is equally famous.Easy walks and the very best tea shops make this a delightful book: £6.95

BEST PUB WALKS IN NORTH DEVON
Dennis Needham

Devon is a tourist paradise, yet few get off the beaten track to explore the delights of country walking and the wealth of tiny Devonshire pubs. Be one of the few! £6.95

EXPLORE THE COAST OF DEVON
Paul Wreyford

"...an inexpensive and handy reference guide for walkers" WESTERN MORNING NEWS.£6.95

PUB WALKS ON DARTMOOR
Laurence Main

Dartmoor may seem forbidding to some, but in the company of Laurence Main, there are many superb walks to enjoy and authentic pubs to visit. £6.95

PUB WALKS IN SOUTH DEVON
Laurence Main

Laurence, with his interest in Earth mysteries and ghostly goings-on, shows that there are all sorts of spirits to be found in Devon - and only some of them in the local hostelries. £6.95

BEST PUB WALKS IN CORNWALL

Laurence Main

Both coastal and countryside walks are to be found in this excellent book, with a Real Ale pub in every village to be visited. £6.95

MYTHS AND LEGENDS OF CORNWALL

Craig Weatherhill & Paul Devereux

The ancient land of Cornwall is steeped in folklore and mystery - all retold by two leading experts - "Superb guide" THE CAULDRON. £6.95

CORNISH PLACE NAMES AND LANGUAGE

Craig Weatherhill

"Probably the most important handbook devoted to the use of the Cornish language in Cornwall's place names" CORNISH WORLD. £6.95

In case of difficulty, or for a free catalogue, please contact: **SIGMA LEISURE, 1 SOUTH OAK LANE, WILMSLOW, CHESHIRE SK9 6AR.**
Phone: 01625-531035; Fax: 01625-536800.
E-mail: sigma.press@zetnet.co.uk .

Web site: http//www.sigmapress.co.uk

VISA & MASTERCARD orders welcome.
Please add £2 p&p to all orders.